THE BEST 100 POEMS OF GWEN HARWOOD

THE BEST 100 POEMS OF GWEN HARWOOD

Published by Black Inc.,
an imprint of Schwartz Books Pty Ltd
22–24 Northumberland Street
Collingwood VIC 3066, Australia
enquiries@blackincbooks.com
www.blackincbooks.com

This edition published in 2022

9781760643652 (paperback)
9781922231864 (ebook)

A catalogue record for this book is available from the National Library of Australia

Cover design by Peter Long
Cover photograph by Deb Morris
Author photograph courtesy of University of Melbourne Archives

CONTENTS

ALTER EGO

Who stands beside me still,
nameless, indifferent
to any lost or ill
motion of mind or will,
whose pulse is mine, who goes
sleepless and is not spent?

Mozart said he could hear
a symphony complete,
its changing harmonies clear
plain in his inward ear
in time without extent.
And this one, whom I greet

yet cannot name, or see
save as light's sidelong shift,
who will not answer me,
knows what I was, will be,
and all I am: beyond
time's desolating drift.

In half-light I rehearse
Mozart's cascading thirds.
Light's lingering tones disperse.
Music and thought reverse
their flow. Beside dark roots
dry crickets call like birds

that morning when I came
from childhood's steady air
to love, like a blown flame,
and learned: time will reclaim
all music manifest.
Wait, then, beside my chair

as time and music flow
nightward again. I trace
their questioning voices, know
little, but learn, and go
on paths of love and pain
to meet you, face to face.

THE WINE IS DRUNK

The wine is drunk, the woman known.
Someone in generous darkness dries
unmanly tears for what's not found
in flesh, or anywhere. He lies
beside his love, and still alone.

Pride is a lie. His finger follows
eye, nostril, outline of the cheek.
Mortal fatigue has humbled his
exulting flesh, and all he'd seek
in a loved body's gulfs and hollows

changes to otherness: he'll never
ravish the secret of its grace.

I must be absent from myself
must learn to praise love's waking face,
raise this unleavened heart, and sever

from my true life this ignorant sorrow.
I must in this gross darkness cherish
more than all plenitude the hunger
that drives the spirit. Flesh must perish
yet still, tomorrow and tomorrow,

be faithful to the last, an old
blind dog that knows the stairs, and stays
obedient as it climbs and suffers.
My love, the light we'll wake to praise
beats darkness to a dust of gold.

IN HOSPITAL

Morning. I dare not stir
for what may wake, for what pain may wake.
My daughter yesterday
unwillingly for my sake
brought here, carried with her
this jar full of odd things,
stones, shells, glass, scavengings
from our last holiday:

sea-toys, child's jewels, rolled
to smooth anonymous shapes. She filled
the jar with water to bring
a gleam back from their chilled
and speechless world. They hold
salt air, soft stone, clear light
and a swallow's ragged flight,
wings closed, continuing

in air between wave and wave.
Arrogant on that shore I raced
with my child. Pain splinters me.
I am cracked like glass. I taste
salt, my own fear, can save
nothing, am ground, degraded
on my own fragments, abraded
featureless. And am free

of pain for a brief space.
A fire-talented tongue will choose
its truth. I do not bear
what's gone, do not refuse
what's yet to come. The grace
of water rinsed, re-made
these stones. My tongue's betrayed
by pain. They speak my prayer.

BEETHOVEN, 1798

To Rex Hobcroft

He sings, often at night; his voice is shocking.
The embarrassed aristocracy are fuel
for his crude wit, and something wild and cruel
flashes through early sweetness. Fate is knocking.
Power lives already in that pockmarked scowl.
When at his improvising someone weeps
he mocks and bellows, "Fool!" His misery keeps,
with easy pace, beside him. Critics howl,
"Bizarre, tormented." Half his life is gone.
Now from your dolphin-hands I learn the strong
leaping of spirit through a temporal sea
of human love and grief. Pain breaks upon
these notes in splintering trills; here, changed to song,
wears the calm aspect of divinity.

THE GLASS JAR

To Vivian Smith

A child one summer's evening soaked
a glass jar in the reeling sun
hoping to keep, when day was done
and all the sun's disciples cloaked
in dream and darkness from his passion fled,
this host, this pulse of light beside his bed.

Wrapped in a scarf his monstrance stood
ready to bless, to exorcize
monsters that whispering would rise
nightly from the intricate wood
that ringed his bed, to light with total power
the holy commonplace of field and flower.

He slept. His sidelong violence summoned
fiends whose mosaic vision saw
his heart entire. Pincer and claw,
trident and vampire fang, envenomed
with his most secret hate, reached and came near
to pierce him in the thicket of his fear.

He woke, recalled his jar of light,
and trembling reached one hand to grope
the mantling scarf away. Then hope
fell headlong from its eagle height.
Through the dark house he ran, sobbing his loss,
to the last clearing that he dared not cross:

the bedroom where his comforter
lay in his rival's fast embrace
and faithless would not turn her face
from the gross violence done to her.
Love's proud executants played from a score
no child could read or realize. Once more

to bed, and to worse dreams he went.
A ring of skeletons compelled
his steps with theirs. His father held
fiddle and bow, and scraped assent
to the malignant ballet. The child dreamed
this dance perpetual, and waking screamed

fresh morning to his window-sill.
As ravening birds began their song
the resurrected sun, whose long
triumph through flower-brushed fields would fill
night's gulfs and hungers, came to wink and laugh
in a glass jar beside a crumpled scarf.

HOME OF MERCY

By two and two the ruined girls are walking
at the neat margin of the convent grass
into the chapel, counted as they pass
by an old nun who silences their talking.

They smooth with roughened hands the clumsy dress
that hides their ripening bodies. Memories burn
like incense as towards plaster saints they turn
faces of mischievous children in distress.

They kneel: time for the spirit to begin
with prayer its sad recourse to dream and flight
from their intolerable weekday rigour.
Each morning they will launder, for their sin,
sheets soiled by other bodies, and at night
angels will wrestle them with brutish vigour.

IN THE PARK

She sits in the park. Her clothes are out of date.
Two children whine and bicker, tug her skirt.
A third draws aimless patterns in the dirt.
Someone she loved once passes by — too late

to feign indifference to that casual nod.
"How nice," *et cetera.* "Time holds great surprises."
From his neat head unquestionably rises
a small balloon ... "but for the grace of God ..."

They stand awhile in flickering light, rehearsing
the children's names and birthdays. "It's so sweet
to hear their chatter, watch them grow and thrive,"
she says to his departing smile. Then, nursing
the youngest child, sits staring at her feet.
To the wind she says, "They have eaten me alive."

O COULD ONE WRITE AS ONE MAKES LOVE

O could one write as one makes love
when all is given and nothing kept,
then language might put by at last
its coy elisions and inept
withdrawals, yield, and yielding cast
aside like useless clothes the crust
of worn and shabby use, and trust

its candour to the urgent mind,
its beauty to the searching tongue.
Safe in the world's great house with all
its loves and griefs, at ease among
its earthly fruits, original
as earth and air, the body learns
peace, while the mind in torment burns

to strip the cloak of daily use
from language. Could one seize and move
the stubborn words to yield and sing,
then one would write as one makes love
and poems and revelations spring
like children from the mind's desire,
original as light and fire.

PRIZE-GIVING

Professor Eisenbart, asked to attend
a girls' school speech night as an honoured guest
and give the prizes out, rudely declined;
but from indifference agreed, when pressed
with dry scholastic jokes, to change his mind,
to grace their humble platform, and to lend

distinction (of a kind not specified)
to the occasion. Academic dress
became him, as he knew. When he appeared
the girls whirred with an insect nervousness,
the Head in humbler black flapped round and steered
her guest, superb in silk and fur, with pride

to the best seat beneath half-hearted blooms
tortured to form the school's elaborate crest.
Eisenbart scowled with violent distaste,
then recomposed his features to their best
advantage: deep in thought, with one hand placed
like Rodin's Thinker. So he watched the room's

mosaic of young heads. Blonde, black, mouse-brown
they bent for their Headmistress' opening prayer.
But underneath a light (no accident
of seating, he felt sure), with titian hair
one girl sat grinning at him, her hand bent
under her chin in mockery of his own.

Speeches were made and prizes given. He shook
indifferently a host of virgin hands.
"Music!" The girl with titian hair stood up,
hitched at a stocking, winked at near-by friends,
and stood before him to receive a cup
of silver chased with curious harps. He took

her hand, and felt its voltage fling his hold
from his calm age and power; suffered her strange
eyes, against reason dark, to take his stare
with her to the piano, there to change
her casual schoolgirl's for a master's air.
He forged his rose-hot dream as Mozart told

the fullness of all passion or despair
summoned by arrogant hands. The music ended,
Eisenbart teased his gown while others clapped,
and peered into a trophy which suspended
his image upside down: a sage fool trapped
by music in a copper net of hair.

LAST MEETING

Shadows grazing eastward melt
from their vast sun-driven flocks
into consubstantial dusk.
A snow wind flosses the bleak rocks,

strips from the gums their rags of bark,
and spins the coil of winter tight
round our last meeting as we walk
the littoral zone of day and night,

light's turncoat margin: rocks and trees
dissolve in nightfall-eddying waters;
tumbling whorls of cloud disclose
the cold eyes of the sea-god's daughters.

We tread the wrack of grass that once
a silver-bearded congregation
whispered about our foolish love.
Your voice in calm annunciation

from the dry eminence of thought
rings with astringent melancholy:
"Could hope recall, or wish prolong
the vanished violence of folly?

Minute by minute summer died;
time's horny skeletons have built
this reef on which our love lies wrecked.
Our hearts drown in their cardinal guilt."

The world, said Ludwig Wittgenstein,
is everything that is the case.
— The warmth of human lips and thighs;
the lifeless cold of outer space;

this windy darkness; Scorpio
above, a watercourse of light;
the piercing absence of one face
withdrawn for ever from my sight.

THE DOUBLE IMAGE

To Rex Hobcroft

We rest here, where no hours
but the sun's time need be kept.
Fossils speak from the rocks
of a time when this land slept
as ocean's floor. The creek
runs clear in its tumbled bed.

Gentle, and light of heart,
your twins kneel by a pool
stirring the water-creatures;
they laugh, as water reshapes,
at each other's wavering features.
Their double image shines
in water, and above:
as if air had the power
of water to reflect,
or earth itself could speak
some loved syllables twice;
they wear with double grace
marks of your singleness
in gesture, form and face.

THE LAST EVENING

Never again will your hand press
  its comfort on my own.
There's nothing of your mortal dress,
  except this motley thrown

lightly away, this piecemeal cloak
  lying unmoved at last
under the hand of time that broke
  bread with us in the past,

enacting day by day our long
  happiness. Tears contract
to salt for ever on my tongue.
  Pitying nurses act

"Leave them alone" in starchy mime.
  Evening comes close. A screen
hints at the hospital's worst crime:
  no one shall make a scene.

Evening: when sorrow walks abroad.
  Vagabond shadows wake,
and, wandering in the spotless ward,
  enter the heart, and shake

hopelessness like a leper's bell.
  Never. Never. No sign
is given, no grace, no miracle.
  Vain, all dreams of a fine

ending, a florid cadence wreathing
  your life's close, with the heart
buoyant, the deathless spirit breathing
  delight that we must part

on earth for a short time to seize
  our rich reward. I see
God on the crucifix, and He's
  dead. Who will comfort me?

Longer than time is the mind's passion,
  and far beyond eyes' field
nebulae stretch. In human fashion
  our human speech will yield

right answers to the questions asked
  on death, on love. But you
lie quiet, ask nothing. Death has masked
  like snow the world I knew.

Evening: caught in a shaft of rose
  he hangs from his pierced hands,
hero or god, whose silence flows
  over earth's darkening lands.

NIGHTFALL

One evening when a genial air
ruffled the jacaranda trees
Professor Kröte spread his square
musician's hands on his plump knees,
and, sighing, sat alone among the uncaring
derelict drunks, and lovers, while the flaring

coat of the river glowed and flamed
with sunset, and declined to drab
monotony, and smokestacks framed
in saffron light rose up to stab
his breast with memories: a yellow sky;
cypress, jet-black; a boy plays "Islamei"

with arrogant skill; his teacher claws
a fine gilt chair with nervous pride —
and then the turbulent applause;
rococo gods and cherubs ride
his winds of promise, and their gilded scrolls
shine in that glittering hall; the Danube rolls

past those high windows in its skin
of sunset.
            "Who would know me now,
a second-rate musician in
an ignorant town? Or tell me how
discords of fading light find and restore
the colours of a day that comes no more?"

So Kröte mused, as if his lost
hope darkened on the water's face.
The poor drunks slept beneath a host
of falling flowers. In light embrace
awaiting night, young lovers moved their tender
hands with instinctive gestures of surrender.

Sleep with its textureless draperies
curtained him. His lean spirit stayed
watchful among the shaken trees
drinking God's peace, and humbly prayed
for daily bread, for one hour when he might
rejoice, that his soul be not required that night.

Kröte, waking from troubled rest,
tossing his wild musician's hair,
feeling the torment leave his breast
and vanish in the gentle air,
knew he must find, in his soul's night, alone,
what more the city held than brick and stone.

AT THE ARTS CLUB

Kröte is drunk, but still can play.
Knick-knacks in shadow-boxes wink
at gewgaws while he grinds away
at Brahms, not much the worse for drink.

The hostess pats her tinted curls.
Sees, yawning surreptitiously,
a bitch in black with ginger pearls
squeezing the local tenor's knee.

Kröte lets the loud pedal blur
a dubious trill. The variations
on Handel's foursquare theme occur
to most as odd manipulations

of something better left alone.
They suffer. Kröte knows they do:
with malice adds some more, his own,
and plays all the repeats right through.

He was expected to perform
a waltz, or something short and sweet.
The coffee's made, the supper's warm,
the ravenous guests would love to eat.

Sober, Kröte's inclined to gloom.
Drunk, he becomes a sacred clown.
He puffs and pounds and shakes the room.
An ill-placed ornament falls down.

A pause. Chairs squeak. The hostess claps,
wrongly — there's still the fugue to play.
Tenor and Ginger Pearls, perhaps
for ever, boldly sneak away.

MONDAY

Kröte sits on the beach at noon
  drinking the blood-red wine.
"Oh how shall I pluck from air some tune
  to match this life of mine?"

A Council notice close at hand
  says liquor is forbidden.
In a damp hollow in the sand
  he keeps his bottle hidden.

A few young mothers come his way.
  They frown at Kröte, jerking
their children past as if to say
  decent men would be working.

Kröte thinks: If I had a child ...
  and dreams himself a creature
with smoky hair, whose spirit's wild
  as wind, whose inmost nature

mirrors his love. The crowding gulls
  rise, as a dumpy likeness
of Kröte's dream, in spectacles,
  stones them. A wave of sickness

shakes him. The child comes close, and hangs
  over him with a grin,
then with her metal spade she bangs
  sharply on Kröte's shin.

Kröte flinches with pain, and scowls,
  "Mädchen, why do you hit me?"
He grabs the lifted spade. She howls
  "Don't let that bad man get me."

The women turn from their affairs.
  The vicious child lets loose a
torrent of lies. Her mother glares
  at Kröte like Medusa.

"Monster! You filthy pervert!" scream
  the child-envenomed jury;
round his condemned retreat they seam
  the tissue of their fury.

In vain this night will Kröte try
  on the rinsed beach to find
his wine, or lose the thoughts that lie
  like stains upon his mind.

WIND

In gloomy Sunday calm the town
rests in the branches' tossing frame.
To empty streets the gulls drops down.
Their nervous arcs of action claim

the eye of that young awkward girl
who's waiting in a flimsy dress
while dry leaves crackle close and swirl
their scarves about her chill distress

until, along the windy street,
her whistling lover strides to bless
her waiting with his joy. They meet
transformed to radiant presences.

Around the fringes of their dream
dance yellow leaves. They kiss, and stare,
indifferent to the gulls that scream
hunger through wintry shires of air.

Professor Kröte walks alone
past their beatitude, and from
his spirit cannot tear his own
barbed instruments of martyrdom,

but suffers, leaning on the wind,
shaking his head as if he tried
beyond its senseless noise to find
some note whose echoes had just died.

FEVER

Kröte lies feverish and sick
in hospital where sterile gleams
of chrome pluck at his aching head.
Pain wrings his hands, a phantom double
out of control. Some fever-trick
beguiles a desolate hour: he dreams
a host of friends come to his bed
with fruit and wine. But who would trouble

to flesh the unstaged reality
of Kröte's dreams? Someone. He wakes
to see one of his pupils standing
close to him, a thin child whose plain
features, unformed as yet, could be
ugly or beautiful. She makes
no secret of her undemanding
worship, is happy to remain

awkwardly, in school uniform,
ignorant of her inmost hunger,
thinking of love as a child may —
gentle kisses and sweets. "I've brought
a gift." As Kröte takes the warm
packet, his chill hand feels a younger
quick-fingered grasp; she tears away
the wrapping. Gift. *Vergiftet.* Caught

between two languages his mind
falters. *Gift.* Poison. Fever wears
his flesh. His sickness raps upon
façades beyond which Nothing grins.
Demons and near-men howl behind
his headache, but the young girl stares
transfixed as if a great light shone
from Kröte's face. A nurse begins

her rounds: sees on his bed the box
of sweets. "You can't have those." His hands
close on the box. A ludicrous
struggle ensues as Kröte holds
harder, frowns like Beethoven, locks
fingers of power. His pupil stands
giggling, while Kröte, furious,
triumphant, glares at the nurse, who scolds

her patient as she would a child,
and, thinking that his pupil is
his daughter, leaves the two alone.
Kröte leans on his pillow, breathing
as if asleep. It seems the wild
mane of his hair is touched. A kiss
light as a wafer? Or his own
imagining? He sleeps. A seething

darkness finds where his life is laid.
Maps of an empty continent,
himself, are drawn in bleeding scrawls.
Keep me, his spirit prays, from ill.
By its own scope the heart's betrayed
to monstrous dreams, and throbs assent:
"I'll make the creature mine." He falls
through a black void, himself, and still

falling wakes into darkness, crying
"Poison!" A tired sister lays
her book aside and jabs his arm.
Rest shall be given where rest is wanted.
Elsewhere this night a child is lying
restless, sure-hearted as she prays
innocently for undreamed-of harm,
then sleeps, certain her prayer is granted.

EBB-TIDE

Now that you have no word for me
I bring your bitter silence here
where the tide rustles from the land
seaward, its whispered meaning clear.
My young son chases, stone in hand,
a sandcrabs' rattling greyblue army.

He stones the scuttling host, and gathers
one crippled prize. Cannot decide
which is its head. As dying claws
tickle his palm, he laughs. The tide
withdraws for his delight. We pause
at every pool. The mind surrenders

its agony to littoral creatures
rocked in the comfort of the shore's
unvarying seasons. A smooth spine
held in my idle fingers scores
a name in sand as the gulls sign
the windless water with your features.

I have one picture of you taken
picnicking somewhere: mountains, clouds
beyond a pier; incredibly blue
water surrounds you, masts and shrouds
pattern unheard-of azure. You
smile there forever. Time has shaken

life from the sea, flung on dry land
bones that got upright, fleshed their wild
sea-creature grins, and learned the weight
of earth. I run beside my child
stoning the crabs with mindless hate.
The sea withdraws from the gold sand.

THE DIAMOND SPARROW

Most handsome of our birds, he'd swell
his fine chest out and give a long
high whistle. Yesterday he died.
I took his corpse and went to tell
the children, and the youngest tried
to warm him. There's no dearth of song

to celebrate the death of birds.
I think now of a prison wall
pockmarked with bullet holes. The stuff
of poetry is man, and words
are all he has, often enough,
in this age. Still, a ritual

was followed for the children's sake:
wrapped in white cloth the creature lay
in slate, and then was burnt. I find
his delicate ashes as I rake
the fire, and watch them whirl away
like ghosts of birds on the chill wind.

REFUGEE

I remember the rough-spoken landscape frayed
by years of upheaval, the towns
unimaginably old, and the thoughtful passion
of the Christ in a church where we prayed.

I remember locked figures in the streets
Duel or embrace, I did not know.
The impetuous gestures of our guide
as we came to that place where the river meets

rock, the savage boldness of the flood.
A voice saying *Freedom* in a tongue
I have forgotten. The wet red sandstone.
My lifelong terror of blood.

I remember the ocean licking at lonely piers
and the scavenged food.
                                        I cannot remember the faces
of father, mother, my sister; only the places
that were not home, and the tears.

BURNING SAPPHO

The clothes are washed, the house is clean.
I find my pen and start to write.
Something like hatred forks between
my child and me. She kicks her good
new well-selected toys with spite
around the room, and whines for food.
Inside my smile a monster grins
and sticks her image through with pins.

The child is fed, and sleeps. The dishes
are washed, the clothes are ironed and aired.
I take my pen. A kind friend wishes
to gossip while she darns her socks.
Scandal and pregnancies are shared.
The child wakes, and the Rector knocks.
Invisible inside their placid
hostess, a fiend pours prussic acid.

Night now. Orion first begins
to show. Day's trivial angers cease.
All is required, until one wins,
at last, this hour. I start to write.
My husband calls me, rich in peace,
to bed. Now deathless verse, good night.
In my warm thighs a fleshless devil
chops him to bits with hell-cold evil.

All's quiet at last: the world, the flesh,
the devils burning in my brain.
Some air of morning stirs afresh
my shaping element. The mind
with images of love and pain
grapples down gulfs of sleep. I'll find
my truth, my poem, and grasp it yet.
  "The moon is gone, the Pleiads set ..."

SUBURBAN SONNET

She practises a fugue, though it can matter
to no one now if she plays well or not.
Beside her on the floor two children chatter,
then scream and fight. She hushes them. A pot
boils over. As she rushes to the stove
too late, a wave of nausea overpowers
subject and counter-subject. Zest and love
drain out with soapy water as she scours
the crusted milk. Her veins ache. Once she played
for Rubinstein, who yawned. The children caper
round a sprung mousetrap where a mouse lies dead.
When the soft corpse won't move they seem afraid.
She comforts them; and wraps it in a paper
featuring: *Tasty dishes from stale bread.*

CHANCE MEETING

I smile. Anger contracts your face.
Two women talking, who might seem
old friends to casual passers-by,
we stand in this familiar place.
Sometimes I meet you in a dream,
here, and all's well. How often I

fashion some god who smiles on me
when smiles are wanting — but such dreams
are faded chromolithotints
reversed from hard reality.
Not love, nor hate, but something streams
between us, as you speak with hints

of knowing this or that which might
hurt me: some brilliance of the mind
that lights us, at whatever cost.
If we were men, perhaps we'd fight,
mop up the blood, let friendship find
more casual ways and not be lost.

You thrash our history for old
misdeeds that hardly bear retracing.
I grin and joke as the words sting.
Really I feel like Archibald
Douglas in heavy armour racing
breathless beside his angry king:

but you're no king, and I'm no knight;
we've no Linlithgow's peace to ride to.
We're women in an elegant war.
The weather goes pathetic; light
turns grey; it's raining. You decide to
drive me. What do you do it for,

knowing too well I know by heart
your bone-clear profile and the way
the hair springs from your brow. We sit
as close as friends, but far apart,
and I'm too close to tears to say
plain words keener than wounding wit:

no one who knows what friendship is
chooses and picks the virtuous;
we love where we must love; so when
we showed ourselves without disguise
friendship itself had chosen us.
I could have hidden from you then

all you reproach me with. You suffer
that knowledge as I suffer still
the self that made my tongue my own
to speak the love I still must offer
whether you wish me well or ill.
You drop me. I walk on alone.

NIGHTFALL

To the memory of Vera Cottew

Houselights waken. It grows late.
Cold flowers wreathe a ruined gate.
    Over it steps a man.
    Wet sand bursts into flame.

He walks on the deserted shore.
His footsteps mark its burning floor.
    Water walks at his heels
    rustling broken shells.

Layer on layer of gold leaf
peels from the sea. I read his grief
    and its weight which can be told
    from the way his body's held.

This nightfall glow, water's soft lapping
he treads away: a fancy wrapping
    on his world's empty box.
    Declared lifeless by his kicks,

breast upward on the rosy sand,
a parable of old raptures and
    their compensating pain
    a seabird lies. The man

turns, and walks, and turns unseeing.
Light fails. Some density of being
    marks him as he walks on
    when the last light is gone.

In Brisbane twenty years ago
I sat with you, watching the glow
    of calm water at nightfall;
    silent, secure in full

acknowledgment of our unending
heritage; earth's beauty mending
    the miseries of time.
    You suffered. I could not come

a thousand miles, being great with child.
I walked in joy. Your cells ran wild.
    Others held you that day
    when you put brightness by.

Beside your easel once you put
poinsettias and halved fruit,
    and smiling said, "See how
    light speaks always of now."

Fruit, flowers. In paint they multiply
the talents of your hand and eye;
    in their still life unite
    vanished and present light.

In deepest solitude we reach
another's. Up and down the beach
    a man walks, bearing in gross
    darkness some mortal loss.

FOUR IMPROMPTUS

To Rex Hobcroft

I

Changed by the fugitive light of dusk
the landscape melts and flows to peace,
but the heart fretting in its husk
of flesh is restless, seeks release.

As a young child I could not bear
to see the sun go down, and I
would pray for endless light; no prayer
could keep the sun firm in the sky

and shadows one by one would claim
my world. At nightfall still, some fear,
some anguish that I cannot name
grips me, and evening finds me here

obscurely troubled, a plain fool
mourning for daylight's transience,
who cannot make of light a tool
to shape joy from the flux of sense.

Wholeness is elsewhere. At this hour
I sense and fear the involving shape
of absence, and a night whose power
the gifts of grace alone escape.

II

Early for my first lesson, afraid to knock,
I waited, an awkward child, outside a room
where scales, while a metronome pulsed like a feverish clock,
unwound their procession of notes; and in the gloom

of that empty hall the sounds turned in my head
to syllables of a language I must make
my own: clear-sounding, as airy and plain as bread
they summoned a hungering child to enter and take

nourishment in a world whose joy transcends
all temporal need, where the heart understands
unquestionable shapes of truth, and mends
its mortal wounds.
                              You enter, and warm your hands

by playing scales, and again as the notes unfold
heart stirs and wakens, waiting to enter in
its passion of sound. I listen, as of old:
this hour will change my life. All's to begin.

III

Those who are lucky find a few:
to the heart's innermost recesses
their words and looks and gestures fall
like light, and this is mutual.

Think of light entering a room:
nothing is asked, and nothing offered;
but mind and eye together wake
to see the commonest objects take

authentic clarity of form,
and fresh from rest the heart embraces
for a brief moment, unafraid,
the stuff of which the world is made.

This day will end. The world will end.
Light changes, and we change and suffer.
But for this hour I offer you,
whose warmth and words and skill renew

the heart, a poem, though words can never
contain, as music does, the unsayable
grace that cannot be defined
yet leaps like light from mind to mind.

IV

Clear, simple as a windless day
calm in its paradise of blue,
when through the quiet of earth it seems
that earth itself will speak to you:

when eyes from every bush and flower
stare into being, and thoughts move
in visions, and love is answered in
the human faces that you love:

clear as a landscape filled with sun
issues this theme, a drift of air
brought into form by mind and hand.
Let heart put off its cloudy care,

rejoice to learn how in the plain
texture of truth its peace is found,
and rest in elemental joy
under this firmament of sound.

IN BRISBANE

By the old bridge in flaring sunlight
a ghost is waiting, with my face
of twenty years ago, to show me
the paths I never can retrace.

Here as of old upon the river
float light's beguiling images.
Over a quilt of blue the branches
bend with domestic tenderness.

Here, to my blood's exalted rhythm,
silly with love I'd pace for hours
sifting the piecemeal revelations
of life and time through falling flowers.

Intemperate ghost, who longed to hazard
the pure space of experience,
to bid unheard-of constellations
form from their joyful elements:

these trees that cannot hold their blossom,
the public handsomeness of stone
remain. Your grand abstractions shimmered
like light on water, and are gone.

My ghost, my self, most intimate stranger
standing beneath these lyric trees
with your one wineglassful of morning
snatched from the rushing galaxies,

bright-haired and satin-lipped you offer
the youth I shall not taste again.
I know, I bear to know, your future
unlooked-for love, undreamed-of pain.

With your untempered spirit shatter
the glass of time that keeps apart
what was and is.
                    Through fractured sunlight
I see a less-than-shadow pass

to light again. A cloud of blossom
drifts on the water's changing face
from the blue trees unfolding summer
above my head in sunlit space.

REVIVAL RALLY

A delirium of shapes rising and falling:
bodies shake with salvation, arms fling wild
in appeal to the ceiling of the Gospel Hall.
A cripple throws her crutch away, revealing
a nightmare leg. A mother lifts her child,
which howls in terror at the preacher's blessing.
The wicked pianist leaps up, confessing
well-rehearsed sins; sits down; integrates all

the abundant noise with luscious harmonies.
Women who wear their makeup with the pathos
of peasant art settle their cardigans.
Their throats are hoarse, bare light bulbs sting their eyes.
They sing in hot, stale air, lapping the bathos
of a sodden hymn. Old adjectives, old rhymes
fondle their tongues. Amen. The cripple climbs
sweating after her crutch. The pianist fans

a shower of tiny insects from the keys.
The miracle of tongues has been withdrawn.
Let there be silence then. It shall inherit
the suburbs, from Eve's unblemished belly raise
a better race. Lights out. Time to shut down.
Outside, a superb nocturne: street by street
the city lifts its lamps, as if to greet
heaven with luminous gestures of the spirit.

DREAMING, WAKING

Last night thinking of you I fell
asleep, and in a dream you came
saying, "Death is a dream. You will
wake, and will find me still the same

as when in Brisbane long ago
we whistled the whole world to heel."
I woke, still in the dream, to know
your mortal presence near, to feel

through skin, through bone, through brain, a weight
of joy: the world contained you still.
In summer gardens trees with great
arms leaned in the wind to spill

their flux and fire of bloom. Inside
your room, in the no-climate light,
against the wall a canvas dried:
a timeless commonplace of bright

flowers that glowed and seemed to burst
in flame. You turned and stared at me,
dissolving, fading as the first
daylight whispered: reality.

The substance of that world is gone.
I know too well what death can take.
Yet still you come through skin, through bone,
through brain — or do I dream I wake?

PAST AND PRESENT

I

A fish on my hook thrashed
in its passion of air, and spiked
my finger clean to the bone.
On the phosphorescent browns
and blacks of the rotting pier
my blood fell drop by drop.
You seized my finger and sucked the wound,
and left my hand in yours
as you spoke of the echoes of pigment:
how sunset gashed the west
and my blood cooled on decaying wood
with the selfsame fading colours.

A painter absorbed in light,
and myself, neither woman nor child —
a nest of self-torturing demons —
we sat until darkness fell
and the luminescent water glowed
with thickets of bristling eyes,
and shoreward the seawind breathed
in ribs of inconstant stone.
Between the pulse of the sea
and the quick pulse of my throbbing wound
I felt your life-bright presence drawing
my inward sight to its point of rest.

II

To Rex Hobcroft

We walk on this peaceful shore
in the excellence of sunlight.
White hawthorn foams round the houses.
I think of Blake's innocent world
where joy sits on every bough
as your daughter paddles beside us,
amazed at the facts of earth:
at the creatures that glide in her shadow;
at the delicate spines of the dead;
at the surface renewing itself
where she scoops with her hands in the water.
In her wake, like a vision in flux,
a torrent of light streams outward,
and under the fingers of wind
small waves start up in a fugue
of water repeating each shape
in manifold overlapping.

When I walked here last, alone,
it was cold, in the late spring
with Orion back in the sky.
It seemed that one long dead
who had walked with me on another shore
came to my side in darkness.

I walked again with that one
who taught me creation was labour,
who took me beyond the range
of salon pictures and coffee-bar poems
to the passionate patience of art.
I think of the fastness of death.
Of Dietrich Bonhoeffer in prison
remembering a theme:
"Sometimes the music heard
in our inward ear surpasses
the beauty of physical sound.
There is something purer about it."
And perhaps it is so with the dead
when they rise in the mind's image
to walk again with the sharpness of life.

We walk in the present sun
talking of canons and fugues,
art's miracle, which is constant:
that hard-worked artifice
should sound innate, and be music still.
What matter if griefs return
with the spiky thrust of spring?
I know that joy will come
as a voice in a fugue returns
to enter and alter the texture
of accumulating seasons.
I feel time lift and lighten
between the peace of the dead
and the living child beside us
who touches the quick of light.
What's grief but the after-blindness
of the spirit's dazzle of love?

A GAME OF CHESS

To John Brodie

Nightfall: the town's chromatic nocturne wakes
dark brilliance on the river; colours drift
and tremble as enormous shadows lift
Orion to his place. The heart remakes
that peace torn in the blaze of day. Inside
your room are music, warmth and wine, the board
with chessmen set for play. The harpsichord
begins a fugue: delight is multiplied.

A game: the heart's impossible ideal —
to choose among a host of paths, and know
that if the kingdom crumbles one can yield
and have the choice again. Abstract and real
joined in their trance of thought, two players show
the calm of gods above a troubled field.

TO ANOTHER POET

I hold in the same thought
a pain now bearable
and what could not be borne.
This evening out of time
we talk: the world is changed
never to be remade
of its old heaviness.

Something that beat in dumb
fury against the glass
of knowing, knows, and is looking
through stillness at this room
where children swarm, whose play
bespeaks our century:
they spread with formal vengeance

armies across the floor.
Across their noise we talk,
drawn to the same enduring
themes with a wakeful joy.
At the fringes of the mind
fragments of thought are stirred
to life, and gather together.

We have no ready-learnt
paraphrase of the world.
Today's love must sustain
today, and no life is made
of manageable stuff.
But this evening I put off
an old tyrannic grief,

and in this usual room,
a place, a field, a world
where children play, I gather
nourishment from another
mind that seeks, and follows
an orbit like my own.
We smile and say goodnight.

LITTORAL

To Rex Hobcroft

Stones rolled in lively anarchy
through centuries of water grind
these hemispheres in softer stone.
I walk along a narrow ledge
of sandstone at the water's edge,
and thought like water takes its own
shape in the hollows of the mind.
A mile across the river lie

houses and streets, a world away,
where daily I put on the same
mask: my familiar, anti-grand
manner, kindly, responsible —
    dry pebbles in an empty skull
    hear the old clichés roll!
                                        No hand
ravished me from the height I claim.
Freedom is power to choose. Each day

I choose my life, choose to be woven
in other lives, and weave my own
threads in a fabric of such weight
it pulls flesh earthward, yet can lift
a breathing animal to swift
flight from the miseries of fate.
How shall the heart's true shape be known,
spirit made manifest? Beethoven

struggled through temporal misery
to find that form. I think of you
playing those late sonatas fashioned
for a world that will outlast the span
of our own lives, where spirit can
speak of itself, press its impassioned
form upon empty air: each new
theme is a new reality.

Proud of their strength, my children take
turns with the heavy pack, and I
walk light, between the seawind's hum
in airshot cliffs and water's bright
network of overlapping light,
through time where past and future come
to the fine edge of clarity:
a world I never can remake,

a world still to be made. I must
suffer, and change, and question all,
wrestle with thought and word, and bind
my speech to earth's own laws to win
the heart's true life at last.
                                        Once in
a bare room, shaken by the wind
when sunlight shivered and a tall
poplar glittered in shifting dust,

heart leapt beyond music, past the span
of human hands and human skill
to affirm *what is*. My children call
across the wind for me to come;
the tide streams through a honeycomb
of rock and air. This littoral
margin of land and water still
vibrates with life, where life began.

ALLA SICILIANA

To O.B. Dunne

Earthbound, I watch the darting swallows.
In shivering reeds the wind is caught.
Bright water bears away the mind's
unravellings of restless thought.

Sunset's clear-speaking light discloses
in the calm eloquence of stone,
the lapsing syllables of water,
the whispering reeds and grasses blown

to quiet at last, to windfall silence,
another tongue, a language learned
by ear, by heart in earliest childhood,
when earth in its own radiance turned

always from nightmare-dark to morning.
I see that lost enchantment wake
in light, on water, and the spirit
like a loved guest on earth can take

its needs and its delights, and wander
freely. The dazzling moments burn
to time again. In simple twilight
water speaks peace, the swallows turn

in lessening arcs. The dry reeds rustle
and part to set the nightwind free.
The heart holds, like remembered music,
a landscape grown too dark to see.

NEW MUSIC

To Larry Sitsky

Who can grasp for the first time
these notes hurled into empty space?
Suddenly a tormenting nerve
affronts the fellowship of cells.
Who can tell for the first time
if it is love or pain he feels,
violence or tenderness that calls
plain objects by outrageous names

and strikes new sound from the old names?
At the service of a human vision,
not symbols, but strange presences
defining a transparent void,
these notes beckon the mind to move
out of the smiling context of
what's known; and what can guide it is
neither wisdom nor power, but love.

Who but a fool would enter these
regions of being with no name?
Secure among their towering junk
the wise and powerful congregate
fitting old shapes to old ideas,
rocked by their classical harmonies
in living sleep. The beggars' stumps
bang on the stones. Nothing will change.

Unless, wakeful with questioning,
some mind beats on necessity,
and being unanswered learns to bear
emptiness like a wound that no
word but its own can mend; and finds
a new imperative to summon
a world out of unmeasured darkness
pierced by a brilliant nerve of sound.

DUST TO DUST

I dream I stand once more
in Ann Street by the old
fire station. The palms
like feather dusters move
idly in stifling air.
The sky's dusted with gold.
A footfall; someone comes;
I cannot speak for love.

We walk in silence past
All Saints'. The dead do rise,
do live, do walk and wear
their flesh. Your exile's done.
So, so, resume our last
rejoicing kiss. Your eyes
flecked with my image stare
in wonder through my own.

Round us air turns to flame.
Ashes rain from the sky.
A firebell clangs and clangs
insanely as I wake
to absence with your name
shaping my lips. I lie
losing the dream that hangs
fading in air. I shake

the last of night away.
These bright motes that define
morning inside my room
hold not one grain of you.
Another sunstruck day
whose moving dust-motes shine
remote from any dream
cannot restore, renew

our laughter that hot night
when by All Saints' we talked
in the brief time we had.
During *Magnificat*
an urchin stopped to write
on the church wall. He chalked
his message: GOD IS MAD.
I say amen to that.

AN IMPROMPTU FOR ANN JENNINGS

Sing, memory, sing those seasons in the freezing
    suburb of Fern Tree, a rock-shaded place
with tree ferns, gullies, snowfalls and eye-pleasing
    prospects from paths along the mountain-face.

Nursing our babies by huge fires of wattle,
    or pushing them in prams when it was fine,
exchanging views on diet, or Aristotle,
    discussing Dr Spock or Wittgenstein,

cleaning up infants and the floors they muddied,
    bandaging, making ends and tempers meet —
sometimes I'd mind your children while you studied,
    or you'd take mine when I felt near defeat;

keeping our balance somehow through the squalling
    disorder, or with anguish running wild
when sickness, a sick joke from some appalling
    orifice of the nightwatch, touched a child;

think of it, woman: each of us gave birth to
    four children, our new lords whose beautiful
tyrannic kingdom might restore the earth to
    that fullness we thought lost beyond recall

when, in the midst of life, we could not name it,
    when spirit cried in darkness, "*I will have …*"
but what? have what? There was no word to frame it,
    though spirit beat at flesh as in a grave

from which it could not rise. But we have risen.
    Caesar's we were, and wild, though we seemed tame.
Now we move where we will. Age is no prison
    to hinder those whose joy has found its name.

We are our own. All Caesar's debts are rendered
    in full to Caesar. Time has given again
a hundredfold those lives that we surrendered,
    the love, the fruitfulness; but not the pain.

Before the last great fires we two went climbing
    like gods or blessed spirits in summer light
with the quiet pulse of mountain water chiming
    as if twenty years were one long dreaming night,

above the leafy dazzle of the streams
    to fractured rock, where water had its birth,
and stood in silence, at the roots of dreams,
    content to know: our children walk the earth.

REED VOICES

She waits, not far from death,
in her old house by the river.
How the reeds multiply!
They move closer each night
surely, their ghostly plumes
nodding to let the white
heron pass to his nest.
Their delicate armies sway
close-whispering, until the break of day.

What is there to besiege
but an old woman lying
alone, past hope or caring,
with voices in her head
"Not all of us shall die
My love, come to my bed,
and I will give you children.
Let us join in love's play,
lock your limbs close until the break of day."

"Mother." A child, afraid.
Great with another child
she rises clumsily.
"My dear, I am close by.
Shall we look from the window?"
"There are flowers in the sky."
"We call them stars, night's flowers
Sleep, sleep, and I will stay
close to your cot until the break of day."

"Mother, it is a daughter.
We shall call her after you."
And that child, bearing children —
her name, her features taken
by wordless naked strangers.
But her life! She feels it shaken
by a strange wind out of time
that stirs the reeds all night.
She hears them whisper until morning light.

Generations of voices
like water-companies streaming
through the shallows of her mind
flash, ripple, and glide on
to healing depths of sleep.
"Children, where have you gone?"
The reeds shake out their plumes.
Their ghost-light armies stay
guarding her sleep until the break of day.

OYSTER COVE

Dreams drip to stone. Barracks and salt marsh blaze
opal beneath a crackling glaze of frost.
Boot-black, in graceless Christian rags, a lost
race breathes out cold. Parting the milky haze
on mudflats, seabirds, clean and separate, wade.
Mother, Husband and Child: stars which forecast
fine weather, all are set. The long night's past
and the long day begins. God's creatures, made
woodcutters' whores, sick drunks, watch the sun prise
their life apart: flesh, memory, language all
split open, featureless, to feed the wild
hunger of history. A woman lies
coughing her life out. There's still blood to fall,
but all blood's spilt that could have made a child.

WINTER QUARTERS

We sit in someone else's house
a-drinking at the dry red wine
after long separation, flaunting
banners of memory with their strange
devices (others watching us
for intimations of some fine
poetic love-death) round the haunting
sense of a time no time can change.

We learn from one involving stare
all men are mortal, and we are
human indeed. The triumphs won
from time remain invisible.
Years that have taught us how to wear
defeat like an old duelling scar
paled to distinction, flash and run
like minutes to this beautiful

half-drunken *now*, where we might be
two captains resting, wearied by
a long campaign, at ease yet still
alert, friends long enough to show
the heart's true gentleness, to see
the mask of day's authority
put by, drinking night's peace until
a word, a look, can say: I know

as I am known. I look. I store
the memory that must serve so long
Feature by feature I record
your ageing face, through which the loved
unageing spirit shines once more
to liberate the pulse of song
in that calm centre where each word
hangs like a waterdrop unmoved

in early quietness, the real
presence of morning globed in light.
Look long and truthfully. Each scar
declares our living worth. Be sure
that the clean wounds of time will heal.
Rejoice in this unwounded night.
The young are beautiful. We are
ourselves, and love, and will endure.

IRIS

Three years with our three sons you worked to build her,
    named for the rainbow, late and lively child
whom the sea fondles. A fresh breeze has filled her.
    Tension and buoyant ease are reconciled

as she puts off the heavy yoke of land
    and takes the wind's light burden in her sails.
Ship-shape; an even keel: we understand
    old clichés truly — sixty pounds of nails

gripping her ribs, six hundredweight of lead
    flourishing water's frail cascading lace.
Age after age the same, still tenanted
    with earth's first creatures, water bears no trace

of time or history on its shining skin.
    Far from the shore where small crabs trim the rotten
scraps from a city's fringes, we begin
    (husband and wife so long we have forgotten

all singularity), our day of rest
    above that element where none sit hand
in hand, salt glitter tossed from crest to crest
    lights nothing of those gulfs where none can stand

upright; here nothing smiles; pity's unknown.
    A crippled gull I found helplessly dying
used its last life to stab me to the bone.
    Some old, lost self strikes from time's shallows, crying

"Beyond habit, household, children, I am I.
    Who knows my original estate, my name?
Give me my atmosphere, or let me die."
    — Give me your hand. The same pure wind, the same

light-cradling sea shall comfort us, who have
    built our ark faithfully. In fugitive
rainbows of spray she lifts, wave after wave,
    her promise: those the waters bear shall live.

NIGHT FLIGHT

In the limbo of middle air
    we cruise, drowned in high cloud,
between somewhere and somewhere
    with the old Electra's loud
whine, and the seat-frames creaking,
and "This is your Captain speaking ..."

Indifferent to night
    the God in the machine
tells us our speed and height,
    names crisply the unseen
landmarks and towns below —
nothing I need to know.

I see those well-known places
    like snatches of old song:
my house, my children's faces;
    late roses left too long
in a rosé bottle, dying.
O, that we two were lying —

O that we two were — Christ,
    what do I want, or need?
Once, when the world sufficed
    I'd sit for hours to read
to a sick child, or spend
evenings, world without end

in children's games, or rest
    like a gentle animal
with a baby at my breast
    watching slow darkness fall,
wrapped in earth's tenderness;
blessed, and with power to bless.

How can this body past
    childbearing lapse and rage,
spirit's fury at last
    quicken, and wreck the cage
of absence, so I stare
across wastes of frozen air? —

barefooted, grave, you stand
    in a room pulsing with wine;
take the glass from my hand,
    and put your hand in mine;
so, like two children playing,
or two court fools displaying

their smiling effigies
    to earnest fools, we dance.
Careless with joy, I seize
    this night's extravagance,
and breathe, as I breathe air,
the world of your despair.

Empty and light, I burn
    with rapture, as of old;
by that heat-lightning learn
    sorrow has taken hold
of this one whom I love.
I feel it, as we move

to *Lucy in the Sky*
    with Diamonds, through my skin.
Absorb it, eye to eye;
    suffer it; drink it in;
clasp it, immediate;
fill with it, bear its weight.

Love whom you will. I've known
    enough of love to know
what flesh holds for its own
    in the molten afterglow:
its gulfs of night, immense,
calm, empty, where each sense

surrenders all, as in
    some rapture of the deep;
where soul and body spin
    through the grand depths of sleep:
so I float, for a brief space,
in the dance, in your embrace.

Suffer my love, as I
    suffer myself, still flying
with Lucy in the sky
    among dazzling visions, lying
in half-sleep in mid-air
between nowhere and nowhere.

What's love but this sustaining
    violence — grains of time
igniting, burning, raining
    through absence as I climb
on stormy air to lie
alone in the black sky.

AT MORNINGTON

They told me that when I was taken
to the sea's edge, for the first time,
I leapt from my father's arms
and was caught by a wave and rolled
like a doll among rattling shells;
and I seem to remember my father
fully clothed, still streaming with water
half comforting, half angry.
And indeed I remember believing
as a child, I could walk on water —
the next wave, the next wave —
it was only a matter of balance.

On what flood are they borne,
these memories of early childhood
iridescent, fugitive
as light in a sea-wet shell,
while we stand, two friends of middle age,
by your parents' grave in silence
among avenues of the dead
with their cadences of trees,
marble and granite parting
the quick of autumn grasses.
We have the wholeness of this day
to share as we will between us.

This morning I saw in your garden
fine pumpkins grown on a trellis
so it seemed that the vines were rising
to flourish the fruits of earth
above their humble station
in airy defiance of nature
— a parable of myself,
a skinful of elements climbing
from earth to the fastness of light;
now come to that time of life
when our bones begin to wear us,
to settle our flesh in final shape

as the drying face of land
rose out of earth's seamless waters.
        I dreamed once, long ago,
        that we walked among day-bright flowers
        to a bench in the Brisbane gardens
        with a pitcher of water between us,
        and stayed for a whole day
        talking, and drinking the water.
        Then, as night fell, you said
        "There is still some water left over."
We have one day, only one,
but more than enough to refresh us.

At your side among the graves
I think of death no more
than when, secure in my father's arms,
I laughed at a hollowed pumpkin
with candle flame for eyesight,
and when I am seized at last
and rolled in one grinding race
of dreams, pain, memories, love and grief,
from which no hand will save me,
the peace of this day will shine
like light on the face of the waters
that bear me away for ever.

THE BLUE PAGODA

An obelisk of Reckitt's blue
crystalline glass, one angle cut
so that, held rightly, it would show
a tall pagoda shining through.
Roof after roof it rose in space
accessible to sight alone,
for when I turned it in my hand
the marvel of the tower was gone.

A child too young to understand
the mysteries of refraction, I
believed one evening I would solve
some trick of image-making light
and see the tall pagodas rising,
star-lofting in the night-blue sky,
doors opening on barbaric gold,
their bells and incense freed from stillness.

And once in feverish sickness dreamed
of ships whose cargoes were pagodas
bearing away house, parents, all,
while I lay choking in the hold
of one last empty ship, becalmed.

Nightfall: those skies that had no theme
but their own deepening blue, are sold
for the clear glare of neon winking;
bold, savage colours pulse like suns
where a child stood, who did not know
suns could set behind other things
than houses, hills, and orange trees,
or the heart grasp, in fading light,
comfort, illumination, built
of echoes and reflections by
one colour at the edge of night.

DAVID'S HARP

Saturday morning. I rehearse
the Sunday hymns, fortissimo,
in the cool twilight of the church,
adding new stops at every verse.
Someone creaks the west door. I know
I am the object of his search,
gazed at, as though from far away.
He must be thirty, if a day.

I turn my seventeen-year-old
profile a trifle heavenwards,
and hastily reduce the sound,
accommodating to his bold
descant on *David's Harp*. The Lord's
house might as well be Circe's ground.
        "With thee all night I mean to stay,
        and wrestle till the break of day."

"With thee all night." So Wesley wrote,
though not with secular intent.
What flourishes that tune will bear!
My tenor wreathes it note by note
in rich Handelian ornament.
Faint burnt-out incense on the air
offends his Presbyterian nose.
He sneezes, stares across the rows

of empty pews between us; still
singing, walks to the organ; stands
beside me; puts his arms around
my waist and squeezes me until
I gasp, then gently lifts my hands
to his, and kisses me. He's sound
of wind. His kiss is long. We share
at last a common need for air.

"Give me one kiss, my bonny lass!"
Vain as a cat, I frown and toss
my head. He watches Brisbane's hot
sunshine, strained through Victorian glass,
lacquer a Station of the Cross.
He scowls and thunders: "Thou shalt not
make any graven images."
But as he bends his head to kiss

the image of his hope, the door
moves with its useful warning creak.
He steps aside. I start to play.
He fills his lungs, and sings once more,
        "Speak to me now, in blessings speak."
A death-pale curate come to pray
kneels, and is forced to find his Lord
through a loud F sharp major chord.

Where's that bright man who loved me, when
there was not much to love? He died
soon after. The undying flow
of music bears him close again,
handsome and young, while I am tried
in time's harsh fires. Dear man, I know
your worth, being now less ignorant of
the nature and the names of love.

NIGHT THOUGHTS: BABY & DEMON

Baby I'm sick. I need
nursing. Give me your breast.
My orifices bleed.
I cannot sleep. My chest
shakes like a window. Light
guts me. My head's not right.

Demon, we're old, old chap.
Born under the same sign
after some classic rape.
Gemini. Yours is mine.
Sickness and health. We'll share
the end of this affair.

Baby, I'm sick to death.
But I can't die. You do
the songs, you've got the breath.
Give them the old soft shoe.
Put on a lovely show.
Put on your wig, and go.

The service station flags, denticulate
plastic, snap in the wind. Hunched seabirds wait

for light to quench the unmeaning lights of town.
This day will bring the fabulous summer down.

Weather no memory can match will fade
to memory, leaf-drift in the pines' thick shade.

All night salt water stroked and shaped the sand.
All night I heard it. Your bravura hand

chimed me to shores beyond time's rocking swell.
The last cars leave the shabby beach motel.

Lovers and drunks unroofed in sobering air
disperse, ghost-coloured in the streetlight-glare.

Rock-a-bye Baby
    in the motel
Baby will kiss
    and Demon will tell.

One candle lights us. Night's cool airs begin
to lick the luminous edges of our skin.

When the bough bends
    the apple will fall
Baby knows nothing
    Demon knows all.

Draw up the voluptuously crumpled sheet.
In rose-dark silence gentle tongues repeat
the body's triumph through its grand eclipse.
I feel your pulsebeat through my fingertips.

Baby's a rocker
    lost on the shore.
Demon's a mocker.
    Baby's a whore.

World of the happy, innocent and whole:
the body's the best picture of the soul
couched like an animal in savage grace.
Ghost after ghost obscures your sleeping face.

My baby's like a bird of day
    that flutters from my side,
my baby's like an empty beach
    that's ravished by the tide.

So fair are you, my bonny lass,
    so sick and strange am I,
that I must lie with all your loves
    and suck your sweetness dry.

And drink your juices dry, my dear,
    and grind your bones to sand,
then I will walk the empty shore
    and sift you through my hand.

And sift you through my hand, my dear,
    and find you grain by grain,
and build your body bone by bone
    and flesh those bones again,

with flesh from all your loves, my love,
    while tides and seasons stream,
until you wake by candle-light
    from your midsummer dream,

and like some gentle creature meet
    the huntsman's murderous eye,
and know you never shall escape
    however fast you fly.

Unhoused I'll shout my drunken songs
    and through the streets I'll go
compelling all I meet to toast
    the bride they do not know.

Till all your tears are dry, my love,
    and your ghosts fade in the sun.
Be sure I'll have your heart, my love,
    when all your loving's done.

FIDO'S PAW IS BLEEDING

Fido's paw is bleeding.
Fido's master finds the cut,
puts a nice clean bandage on,
gives his pet a slice of meat.

Fido's paw is hurting.
Fido cannot offer proof.
Fido's master tries to ease it
when his dog begins to whimper
how could he withhold belief?

Master's heart is broken.
Master's mistress left his roof.
Did she find his house oppressive?
Who can tell — she would not speak,
simply packed her gear and left.
Polly screeches, "Shut your beak!"
Polly isn't talking sense.

Fido's paw is better,
but he whimpers round the house.
Who could teach him this pretence?
Polly goes on screeching.
Master writes a lyric poem
so his pain is manifest.
Polly scatters seed and swears.
Master's mistress taught the bird
language hardly fit for use.

Fido in his kennel
makes no claims about the world.
Master gets a blanket,
throws it over Polly's cage.
Out of doors the rising moon
flames above earth's darkening rim
lifts a yellow eye aloft.
Master in his lonely room
counts the wingbeats of his pain
pours another glass of wine

on the dryness of his song.
Wonders where it all went wrong.

"THOUGHT IS SURROUNDED BY A HALO"

— *Ludwig Wittgenstein, Philosophical Investigations 97*

Show me the order of the world,
the hard-edge light of this-is-so
prior to all experience
and common to both world and thought,
no model, but the truth itself.

Language is not a perfect game,
and if it were, how could we play?
The world's more than the sum of things
like moon, sky, centre, body, bed,
as all the singing masters know.

Picture two lovers side by side
who sleep and dream and wake to hold
the real and the imagined world
body by body, word by word
in the wild halo of their thought.

FATHER AND CHILD

I BARN OWL

Daybreak: the household slept.
I rose, blessed by the sun.
A horny fiend, I crept
out with my father's gun.
Let him dream of a child
obedient, angel-mild —

old No-Sayer, robbed of power
by sleep. I knew my prize
who swooped home at this hour
with daylight-riddled eyes
to his place on a high beam
in our old stables, to dream

light's useless time away.
I stood, holding my breath,
in urine-scented hay,
master of life and death,
a wisp-haired judge whose law
would punish beak and claw.

My first shot struck. He swayed,
ruined, beating his only
wing, as I watched, afraid
by the fallen gun, a lonely
child who believed death clean
and final, not this obscene

bundle of stuff that dropped,
and dribbled through loose straw
tangling in bowels, and hopped
blindly closer. I saw
those eyes that did not see
mirror my cruelty

while the wrecked thing that could
not bear the light nor hide
hobbled in its own blood.
My father reached my side,
gave me the fallen gun.
"End what you have begun."

I fired. The blank eyes shone
once into mine, and slept.
I leaned my head upon
my father's arm, and wept,
owl-blind in early sun
for what I had begun.

Forty years, lived or dreamed:
what memories pack them home.
Now the season that seemed
incredible is come.
Father and child, we stand
in time's long-promised land.

Since there's no more to taste
ripeness is plainly all.
Father, we pick our last
fruits of the temporal.
Eighty years old, you take
this late walk for my sake.

Who can be what you were?
Link your dry hand in mine,
my stick-thin comforter.
Far distant suburbs shine
with great simplicities.
Birds crowd in flowering trees,

sunset exalts its known
symbols of transience.
Your passionate face is grown
to ancient innocence.
Let us walk for this hour
as if death had no power

or were no more than sleep.
Things truly named can never
vanish from earth. You keep
a child's delight for ever
in birds, flowers, shivery-grass —
I name them as we pass.

"*Be your tears wet?*" You speak
as if air touched a string
near breaking-point. Your cheek
brushes on mine. Old king,

your marvellous journey's done.
Your night and day are one

as you find with your white stick
the path on which you turn
home with the child once quick
to mischief, grown to learn
what sorrows, in the end,
no words, no tears can mend.

THE LION'S BRIDE

I loved her softness, her warm human smell,
her dark mane flowing loose. Sometimes stirred by
rank longing laid my muzzle on her thigh.
Her father, faithful keeper, fed me well,
but she came daily with our special bowl
barefoot into my cage, and set it down:
our love feast. We became the talk of town,
brute king and tender woman, soul to soul.

Until today: an icy spectre sheathed
in silk minced to my side on pointed feet.
I ripped the scented veil from its unreal
head and engorged the painted lips that breathed
our secret names. A ghost has bones, and meat!
Come soon my love, my bride, and share this meal.

A MUSIC LESSON

Kröte's not well. His mood is bloody.
A pupil he can hardly stand
attacks a transcendental study.
— Lord, send me one real pianist.
Soul of a horse! He shapes her hand
and breathes apologies to Liszt.

"Reflect: in order to create
we must know how to. Think about
the balance between height and weight,
shoulder to fingertip; a hanging
bridge, resilient, reaching out
with firm supports. Let's have no banging!

"Playing begins inside your brain.
Music's much more than flesh and bone.
Relax, and listen. If you strain
your muscles *here* and *here* contract.
You get a stiff, unlovely tone."
His pupil says, "Is that a fact?"

She plays the passage louder, faster;
indeed deliberately tries
to infuriate her music master.
"The year that Liszt was born, a comet
blazed over European skies."
"Am I to draw conclusions from it?

"And, if so, what?" the tyro sneers.
— Cold heart, stiff hands. How to explain?
"When a new genius appears
it's like that fiery head of light
drawing us in its golden train.
Now, shall we try to get it right?

Does it give you no pride to say
'My teacher's teacher learned from Liszt?'
Feel in your hands, before you play,
the body's marvellous architecture:
the muscles between hand and wrist
kept flexible; now try to picture

"the finger forming, from the point
where it rests on the key, an arc
curving through every finger-joint,
supporting the whole arm's free weight.
Now the least effort makes its mark.
The instrument can sing."

"I'm late,"

the pupil whines. The lesson's over.
The teacher pours himself a gin,
pats the piano like a lover
(— Dear mistress, we're alone once more).
Liszt, with his upper lip gone in,
beams from the cover of a score.

Abbé, forsooth! A toast to you,
old friend, old fiend in monkish dress.
I know you had your off days too.
At Schumann's, Clara said, you played
his work so badly once (confess!)
that only her good manners made

her sit in silence in that room.
— Have mercy on all pianists,
Architect of the world, of whom
I ask that I may live to see
Halley's Comet.
If God exists
then music is his love for me.

OYSTER COVE PASTORALS

I TO THE MUSE

My fowls with heroes' names,
Hector, Achilles, Ajax,
crow me out to the pasture.
Helios gilds their plumes.
Fossickers in the rye,
they trust me with the axe.

If by some chance I wrote
a fine immortal poem
it would have a mortal theme.

All that excess of life
in museums of the mind
still there to contemplate!

Light fits a world together
from fragments of a dream:
another place, another
morning; a motto: *Summa
Supremo*, best and ablest.
Some happiness is forecast.

What consent do we ever
give to dreams that embrace us
with the energy of art?
Why do you come at morning
when frosty air is burning
my empty arms? I split

wood, light the day's fire,
warm my body at flame
invisible in sunlight.
That brief motto in Latin,
on what door was it written?
Tell me, what is your name?

II HIGH NOON

Ocean, heaven, the same colour.
Bruny lies between
unruffled sky, unclouded water.
Colours of solitude surround us.
Shadows of gentle green
brush the planes of thigh and shoulder.

In this room a whispered name will answer
the soft-spoken address
of eye and lip and loving gesture.
No need for language, the great mirror,
when the body's genius
lights us past logic into rapture.

Instrument and interpreter,
we are one: talk idly, improvise.
    "How will you paint me this green air
    and the distant fields' autumnal shimmer?"
    — As you will sing a dream of leaves
    through which the heavens fall like water.

III EVENING: "ET IN ARCADIA EGO"

Even here, in Arcady, are graves:
the mortal part of Gabriel Fur;
Big White the leghorn; old Artemis,
smallest of bantam hens, and her
arch-enemy the feral cat;
the odd wren, the bright pardalote
and the fantail with his cinnamon breast
who stooped to fly clean through the house
and struck the mystery of glass;
gone to their everlasting rest.

Look, where the grass grows more intense:
a bluetongue's skeleton recounts
his lost encounter with the fence.
If there were reason to give thanks
I'd say, earth gathers in her children
and all are equal, born again.
new dreams fire upwards in her thought —
that's earth's religion: fowl to iris,
cat to fresh catmint, lizard to grass,
grass back to geese in a fresh start.

Insect-spires, grass-heads, complex clouds:
nothing but light and surfaces
as the day dies. Autumnal shades
make substance possible. Come close,
friends, lovers, nightfall-visitors
from earlier times. My body wears
the light and substance of the dead.
Daughters and sons of Artemis
come close, and you, my hungry geese.
Here's wheat. The living must be fed.

A LITTLE NIGHT MUSIC

Listen, I will remind you
of what you have never known.
That's what our dreams are for,
and I will be your dream,
a ravishing latecomer
under your handsome skin.
Late, late this night I'll find you

where nothing has a name,
where any page you turn
will long have lost its meaning.
Remember me, while music
melts you to understanding.
Sleep, while new planets burn,
and I will be your dream.

Frost ghosts autumnal pastures.
Though my step is light, my geese
sound their alarm, the plover
scream at me, an intruder
in sleepless fields, and over
your absence measureless
silence extends the stars.

DEATH HAS NO FEATURES OF HIS OWN

Death has no features of his own.
He'll take a young eye bathed in brightness
and the raging cheekbones of a raddled queen.
Misery's cured by his appalling taste.
His house is without issue. He appears
garlanded with lovebirds, hearts and flowers.
Anything, everything.
He'll wear my face and yours.
Not as we were, thank God. As we shall be
when we let go of the world, late ripe fruit falling.
What we are is beyond him utterly.

BEYOND METAPHOR

Sometimes I'm gripped by poems so sad and awful
I could not write them down. They're like those dreams
you have of irremediable anguish
but can't recount, though you were there, you suffered
your lost love's pain, your child's unanswered cry.
Only Mozart, perhaps, found the right tone
to make things bearable. Who was it said
of the end of the *Tractatus*: What you can't say
you can't say, and you can't whistle it either.

EVENING, OYSTER COVE

"What is history to me? Mine is the first and only world"
— Wittgenstein

The early painters had it right:
  closefisted gums, hills humped on hills,
chill distances where the heart might
  stop in its tracks for loneliness.

Calm tide. My solitary wake
  arrows the glistening waterskin.
Crows, bound for Bruny. Wingbeats make
  the sound of runners breathing, in

their firm compacted paths of air.
  Sunset pours golden syrup on
the northern sandstone. Treetops flare
  briefly, and then the sun is gone.

My geese call from the western rise —
  Babydoll, Fido, Stagolee —
the haunting wildness of their cries
  mocks well-fed domesticity.

This elbow of the shallow bay
  crooked an unchilded dying race
whose liquid language ebbed away.
  Shadows forgather in this place:

Jackey, Patty, Queen Caroline,
  Lalla Rookh — white contemptuous names
cloaked the heartsickness of decline.
  The Governor brought them children's games,

toys, marbles, balls. Let history write
  death after hopeless death. The sea's
a sheet of melancholy light.
  Herons half made of shadow seize

their meal, like necromancers search
  obscuring crystal for a sign.
My boat grounds gently on the beach.
  Home to books, fire and chilled white wine.

Ghosts of the night mist, set me free.
  Forgive, until the past is called
wisdom, and history can be
  told in some last redeeming world.

RETURN OF THE NATIVE

The big house is turned into flats, the last camphor laurel
cut down, alas; the street paved, the cool weatherboard suburb
gone trendy with fancy brick; but new roses spill
their old abundance of scent, and across the kerb

as if this were a film, a Mintie wrapper blows.
So cut to two freckled children unwrapping Minties
in their camphor laurel house, and from wide windows
let the sounds of teacups and voices and laughter rise.

It is late afternoon, and the towering cumulus gather
over city, suburb and treehouse as everyone tells
silly stories. A pause. A rich baritone voice is clear:
"Well, a gentleman knows where he is if the police own the brothels."

The grown-ups shriek, and repeat the curious line.
Heaven cracks open. The children run, drenched, inside,
and the girl, who learns like a parrot, repeats it again
and is slapped into tears without knowing how she has offended.

And Freddy, who said it while managing his tea
with his hand and his hook says, "She didn't understand,"
and talks about Little Pitchers and says he's sorry.
(He told me once: "When the Germans shot off my hand

"God gave me this hook, it's much better for carrying parcels."
I believed the curving steel grew out of his arm.)
But it's time for some good old songs, and music quells
the world's injustice, and clears away the storm.

> My taxi is waiting. The driver puts down his book.
> It's Volume Two of the brick-red paperback Popper.
> I say, "Full Marx?" He grins, "Half. Have you had a good look?
> Was that your old home? Do you like what they've done to her?
>
> "Do you like what they've done to this old State of yours?
> I'm a useless M.A. It's no use whingeing, but.
> You can't sing hymns in the park, and the police own the parlours.
> But I've a sick wife and a kid, so I keep my mouth shut.

"Ban Uranium, one bald tyre, they'll have you off.
If you're sporting a Jesus Saves they'll let you go
without tyres or lights. You'd better go back down south."
I remember Freddy singing "My old Shako",

and would like to say, he'd given a hand for freedom
and would use his hook if anyone threatened his rights.
But the truth is, he'd have voted to build the Bomb
and to clean the long-haired larrikins out of the streets.

Turn like a jewel that small clear scene in your head:
cloud-blaze, leaf-glitter, loved faces, a radiant voice
singing "Fifty years ago ..." Though you summon the dead
you cannot come as a child to your father's house.

A QUARTET FOR DOROTHY HEWETT

I TWILIGHT

Twilight. Field-mouse light. They rustle
in shadowy palaces of hay.
My old cat, Mr Gabriel Fur,
would hunt to keep the mice away
and like a Harlem Globetrotter
juggle his prizes in the air.

Let the mice fear the owl's soft rush
now their lithe enemy is gone
to nourish a viburnum bush.
On his last night on earth he came
to grizzle gently at my door,
then lay beside me, fur to skin.

Did he recall who killed Cock Robin
when we rose up to earliest birdsong?
"We do not live to experience death,"
said my favourite philosopher
(thinking perhaps about his own).
Tell me what I experience, then,

when I wake to open the house door
hearing a cry I cannot hear,
or when I walk in the scythed field
watching the world give up its light,
and feel ghost-footed at my back
a presence in the rustling stack.

II GOOSE-GIRL

Darkness my refuge, sleep my consolation
hold me a moment on the crest of sunrise.
Out of the false lucidity of dreams I
    know myself waking.

Now I will walk as if you were beside me
hearing the birds' ancestral incantations.
Light turns familiar landscape to a spectral
    anguish of strangeness.

We were like princes choosing their disguises,
meeting at last in joyful recognition,
laughing unmasked at life, the royal game, whose
    rules are all fatal.

Mantled in snow my white, my grey geese nested.
Now they walk safely with their golden children
knowing the hand that feeds them is immortal:
    I am their goddess.

Where are you now, who came through dream and darkness
bodied in light, whom light dissolves to absence?
How will you know me, barefoot in the pasture,
    dressed as a goose-girl?

Under the poem of words there shines another,
like a gold flagon arrogantly buried
by one who knows that earth itself will yield it
    to the true lover.

III A SIMPLE STORY

A visiting conductor
    when I was seventeen,
took me back to his hotel room
    to cover the music scene.

I'd written a composition.
    Would wonders never cease —
here was a real musician
    prepared to hold my piece.

He spread my score on the counterpane
    with classic casualness,
and put one hand on the manuscript
    and the other down my dress.

It was hot as hell in The Windsor.
    I said I'd like a drink.
We talked across gin and grapefruit,
    and I heard the ice go clink

as I gazed at the lofty forehead
    of one who led the band,
and guessed at the hoarded sorrows
    no wife could understand.

I dreamed of a soaring passion
    as an egg might dream of flight,
while he read my crude sonata.
    If he'd said, "That bar's not right,"

or, "Have you thought of a coda?"
    or, "Watch that first repeat,"
or, "Modulate to the dominant,"
    he'd have had me at his feet.

But he shuffled it all together,
    and said, "That's *lovely*, dear,"
as he put it down on the washstand
    in a way that made it clear

that I was no composer.
    And I being young and vain,
removed my lovely body
    from one who'd scorned my brain.

I swept off like Miss Virtue
    down dusty Roma Street,
and heard the goods trains whistle
    WHO? WHOOOOOO? in aching heat.

IV DOROTHY, READING IN HOBART

Lustrous angel, who, if I cried, would hear me,
I call you woman, goddess, muse.
In your dress like the blue between clouds
come out of Tartarus singing
the worst of truth in your voice of shadow.

Truth is humbling. Truth is the last tram
you have to catch, and strap-hang, or not get home.
Truth is the watchman running to King David
with news to weep at, words to tighten harpstrings
like plucked hair. Truth's a court for owls,
a motel room where nymphs and satyrs
howl for nembutal, reclining
in odd conjunction, now-and-never
coupling their life sentences.
Truth will dash out our teeth.

Sing the love-letters never posted,
the lovely game where art is wasted.
Voice of lustre, voice of shadow,
sing the brightness turned to sadness,
death of the suburbs, death of habit,
spirits bowed in milky sweetness,
sing Tennysonian afternoons
when history sighed and harvests parted
over most unhappy shades.

A woman still as a Dutch painting
takes her pen, the old-gold light
cracks itself to mirror-splinters.

Charm with your haunting vox humana
Merlin from his malign enchantment.
Melt the black frost, mysterious angel.
Heaven's long emptied of its gods.
Fill the void with a woman's voice.

NAKED VISION

I was sent to fetch an eye
promised for a fresh corneal graft.
At the doctor's rooms nurse gave me
a common paper bag;
in that, a sterile jar;
in that, the disembodied eye.

I sat in Davey Street
on a low brick garden wall
and looked. The eye looked back.
It gazed, lucid and whole,
from its colourless solution.
The window of whose soul?

Trees in St David's Park
refreshed the lunchtime lovers:
riesling gold, claret dark;
late flowers flaunted all colours.
But my friend and I had eyes
only for one another.

In flawless solitude
it stared, blue as the sky.
Nothing seemed out of range
of our crystalline exchange.
The longing in that eye
will haunt me till I die.

IN PLATO'S CAVE

This darkness holds us like an open hand
which earth could shut. It is the guide's poor jest:
"A dollar to get out." Nobody moves.
Then light. I see your burnt-out profile clearly
against the cloudy coronal of your breath.
It's chill here, always. Water's the one sound.
There's moisture everywhere like sweatshine glossing
bodies in nakedness. Columns on all sides
and nature's genial clefts. I like her jokes:
valances and transparent shawls of rock,
King Solomon's archaic head in limestone —
master of women, and wisdom of a kind.
Upwards, like Orpheus. You'll not look back.
You know too well I'll follow in your track.

THE SECRET LIFE OF FROGS

Mr Gabriel Fur, my Siamese,
brings to the hearth a Common Toadlet,
Crinia tasmaniensis.
Mice are permitted, frogs forbidden.
It will live. I carry it outside.
Its heartbeat troubles my warm hand
and as I set it down I see
two small girls in a warmer land.

> My friend Alice and I would sit
> cradling our frogs behind the tankstand.
> Other fathers would talk about
> the Great War. Mine would only say,
> "I used to be a stretcher-bearer."
> Not seen, not heard, in childhood's earshot
> of the women on the back veranda,
> we knew about atrocities.
> Some syllables we used as charms:
> Passchendaele   Mons   Gallipoli.

We knew about Poor George, who cried
if any woman touched her hair.
He'd been inside a brothel when
the Jerries came and started shooting.
(We thought a brothel was a French
hotel that served hot broth to diggers.)
The girl that he'd been with was scalped.
Every Frog in the house was killed.

Well, that was life for frogs. At school
the big boys blew them up and spiked them.
One bully had the very knife
with which his father killed ten Germans —
twenty — a hundred — numbers blossomed.
Dad the Impaler! making work
for the more humble stretcher-bearers.

In safety by the dripping tankstand
our frogs with matchstick hands as pale
as the violet stems they lived among
cuddled their vulnerable bellies
in hands that would not do them wrong.

MOTHER WHO GAVE ME LIFE

Mother who gave me life
I think of women bearing
women. Forgive me the wisdom
I would not learn from you.

It is not for my children I walk
on earth in the light of the living.
It is for you, for the wild
daughters becoming women,

anguish of seasons burning
backward in time to those other
bodies, your mother, and hers
and beyond, speech growing stranger

on thresholds of ice, rock, fire,
bones changing, heads inclining
to monkey bosom, lemur breast,
guileless milk of the word.

I prayed you would live to see
Halley's Comet a second time.
The Sister said, When she died
she was folding a little towel.

You left the world so, having lived
nearly thirty thousand days:
a fabric of marvels folded
down to a little space.

At our last meeting I closed
the ward door of heavy glass
between us, and saw your face
crumple, fine threadbare linen

worn, still good to the last,
then, somehow, smooth to a smile
so I should not see your tears.
Anguish: remembered hours:

a lamp on embroidered linen,
my supper set out, your voice
calling me in as darkness
falls on my father's house.

CLASS OF 1927

SLATE

Quite often in some trendy quarter
the passion to redecorate
those areas concerned with water
results in an expanse of slate.
Cork tiling's warmer, vinyl's neater.
Slate's forty dollars a square metre.
In kitchen, laundry, loo, I see
the stuff the State School gave us free,
and very soon my morbid, chronic
nostalgia swells to recreate
slate-pencil's piercing squeal on slate,
beloved of all those bored demonic
infants whose purpose was to make
mischief purely for mischief's sake.

We sat, ranked by examination,
those with the best marks at the back.
In undisguised discrimination
at the front sat the dim, the slack,
where they could not converse or fiddle;
and in the undistinguished middle
the hard triers, the fairly bright
laboured to get their set work right
not out of any love of study
but simply to escape the cane.
Somehow the teacher knew whose brain
was cleared by stirring, whose was muddy.
One vacant lad, condemned to go
from year to year in the front row,

was said to have three skulls, poor creature.
Everyone liked to feel his head
and demonstrate its curious feature:
ridge after ridge of bone instead
of brain. Bonehead was oddly charming.
His eagerness was so disarming

the whole class used him as a pet
though he was likely to forget
between instruction and retrieval
the object he was sent to find.
No angst stirred his unleavened mind.
He beamed, and hummed, and knew no evil.
The doctor's son, a clever skite,
found inexpressible delight

in cruelty. This boy collected,
or stole, unpleasant instruments;
with these, at playtime, he dissected
lizards and frogs, or spiked their vents
to see how long they took in dying.
One day the class, kept in for sighing
when Sir set homework, heard a squeak.
Being on our honour not to speak
while Sir was briefly absent (bearing
his cane as always) we turned round
and witnessed, as the source of sound,
a captive mouse, its torturer swearing
because the victim tried to bite.
The back row, silent out of fright,

did nothing, and the middle section
saw, but pretended not to look.
Bonehead, after a brief inspection,
stopped smiling; turned again and took
his slate out of its slot; descended
in fury, and with one blow ended
the wanton vivisector's sport.
Then revolution of a sort
broke out. The stricken head was gory.
We stamped and cheered our hero on.
The unhappy mouse was too far gone
to benefit from Bonehead's glory,
or squeak for victory, or curse
the arrangement of this universe.

When Sir returned the class was sitting
so quietly he racked his wits
and stroked his cane and walked round hitting
his leg, but didn't find the bits
of slate we hid in hasty cleaning.
Nor did he grasp the hidden meaning
of some congealing drops of red.
"Where did you get that bloody head?"
"Knocked it." "Go home. That cut needs dressing."
Our golden silence filled the room.
We sat preparing to resume
our work as if it were a blessing
to write on slate, for Sir to see,
the conjugation of *to be.*

THE SPELLING PRIZE

Every Child's Book of Animal Stories.
To compete, we stood on the wooden forms
that seated four in discomfort.
When you missed your word, you sat down
and wrote it out twenty times.
At last only two were left:
Ella and I, who had sailed
past *ghost*, *nymph*, *scheme*, *flight*, *nephew*,
the shoals of o - u - g - h
and i before e, stood waiting
for the final word. Whoever
put her hand up first when Sir
announced it, could try to spell it.
A pause, while Sir went outside.
Some of the girls started hissing,
"Give Ella a chance. Let her win."

Through the window I saw the playground
bare as a fowlyard, the ditch
in a paddock beyond where frogs
lived out whatever their life was
before the big boys impaled them
on wooden skewers, a glint

from a roof in the middle distance
that was Ella's home. I had been there

the week before, when my grandmother went
to take their baby, the ninth,
my brother's old shawl. Ella coaxed me
to a ramshackle tinroofed shed
where her father was killing a bull calf.
A velvety fan of blood
opened out on the concrete floor
as one of her brothers pumped the forelegs:
"You do this to empty the heart."

The father severed the head, and set it
aside on a bench where the eyes, still trusting,
looked back at what had become
of the world. It was not the sight
of the entrails, the deepening crimson
of blood that sent me crying
across the yard, but the calf's eyes watching
knife, whetstone, carcase, the hand that fed.

Ella followed. "I'll show you my toys."
In that house where nobody owned
a corner, a space they might call their own,
she kept two old dolls in a shoebox.
Below me the whispers continued:
"Let Ella win the prize."
Why, now, does memory brood
on Sir's return, and the moment

when he put down his cane and smoothed
his hair grease-tight on his skull
and snapped out the last word: MYSTIC,
a word never found in our Readers.
My innocent hand flew up.
Sheer reflex, but still, I knew it,
and knew I could slip in a k
or an i for a y and lose,

but did not, and sixty years
can't change it; I stand in the playground
and the pale dust stirs as my friends
of the hour before yell "Skite!"
and "Showoff!" and "Think you're clever!"
They gather round Ella, who turns
one hurt look from her red-rimmed eyes
at my coveted, worthless prize.

RELIGIOUS INSTRUCTION

The clergy came in once a week for Religious Instruction.
Divided by faith, not age, we were bidden to be,
(except for the Micks and a Jew) by some curious deduction
Presbyterian, Methodist, Baptist or C of E.

The Micks were allowed to be useful, to tidy the playground.
But Micah, invited to join them, told Sir "They'd only
give me a hiding", and stayed inside; moved round
as he chose with his book of Hebrew letters, a lonely

example, among the tender lambs of Jesus,
of good behaviour. Handsome as a dark angel
he studied while the big boys laboured to tease us
with hair-tweak, nib-prick, Chinese burns, as the well

of boredom overflowed in games of noughts
and crosses, spitballs, and drawings so obscene
if Sir had found them they'd have earned us six cuts.
"You give me real insight into original sin,"

said one minister in despair, intercepting some verses
describing him as Old Swivelneck. Beaked like a sparrowhawk
he clawed at his collar and singled me out from his class.
I feared his anger rightly, feared he would talk

to our headmaster, or Sir. I stood in disgrace.
Then a quiet voice from the back interrupted his wrath:
"*I am ready to forgive.*" "Who said that? Stand up in your place!"
Micah stood. "It was said by the Lord God of Sabaoth."

Then we heard the monitor's footsteps. Saved by the bell!
In a tumult of voices we spilled into sunlight to play,
a host of rejoicing sinners, too young to feel
original darkness under that burning day.

THE TWINS

Three years old when their mother died
in what my grandmother called
accouchement, my father labour,
they heard the neighbours intone
"A mercy the child went with her."

Their father raised them somehow.
No one could tell them apart.
At seven they sat in school
in their rightful place, at the top
of the class, the first to respond
with raised arm and finger-flick.

When one gave the answer, her sister
repeated it under her breath.
An inspector accused them of cheating,
but later, in front of the class,
declared himself sorry, and taught us
a marvellous word: *telepathic*.

On Fridays, the story went,
they slept in the shed, barred in
from their father's rage as he drank
his dead wife back to his house.
For the rest of the week he was sober
and proud. My grandmother gave them
a basket of fruit. He returned it.
"We manage. We don't need help."

They could wash their own hair, skin rabbits,
milk the cow, make porridge, clean boots.

Unlike most of the class I had shoes,
clean handkerchiefs, ribbons, a toothbrush.
We all shared the schoolsores and nits
and the language I learned to forget
at the gate of my welcoming home.

One day as I sat on the fence
my pinafore goffered, my hair
still crisp from the curlers, the twins
came by. I scuttled away
so I should not have to share
my Saturday sweets. My mother
saw me, and slapped me, and offered
the bag to the twins, who replied
one aloud and one sotto voce,
"No thank you. We don't like lollies."

They lied in their greenish teeth
as they knew, and we knew.
                                        Good angel
give me that morning again
and let me share, and spare me
the shame of my parents' rebuke.

If there are multiple worlds
then let there be one with an ending
quite other than theirs: leaving school
too early and coming to grief.

Or if this is our one life sentence,
hold them in innocence, writing
Our Father which art in Heaven
in copperplate, or drawing
(their work being done) the same picture
on the backs of their slates: a foursquare
house where a smiling woman
winged like an angel welcomes
two children home from school.

BONE SCAN

"Thou hast searched me and known me. Thou knowest my downsitting and mine uprising" — Psalm 139

In the twinkling of an eye,
in a moment, all is changed:
on a small radiant screen
(honeydew melon green)
are my scintillating bones.
Still in my flesh I see
the God who goes with me
glowing with radioactive
isotopes. This is what he
at last allows a mortal
eye to behold: the grand
supporting frame complete
(but for the wisdom teeth),
the friend who lives beneath
appearances, alive
with light. Each glittering bone
assures me: you are known.

THE NIGHT WATCH

I am lying like a creature
from outer space, equipped
for sound and colour vision,
in a capsule of discomfort.
Tubes issue from my body,
one taking, one receiving.

Here and there a window
in the hospital, the space ship,
glows and returns to blankness.
The night crew keep their stations.
Who can make sense of pain
with stars and clouds obscured

in a near-but-never darkness:
the backsides of old buildings
and the Savings Bank sign turning,
symbol of some bizarre
religion of this planet —
Invest and find salvation.

Save and be saved. No use
to me, I can save nothing.
Only watch, in my sleepless
journey towards a grounding
I dare not think about,
the neon sign revolving.

I know a bank … where
the wild thyme grows … indeed
time has grown wild and warped
near the black hole of oblivion:
mind beaten, body showing
its true colours to strangers.

O that tongue of cadmium red
in one of Miro's paintings!
Salveo, I am well.
Salvus, well, sound, unharmed,
entire, whole, safe, uninjured.
And *salvia*, scarlet sage —

what sage would lie here playing
intellectual variations
for a night, a thousand hours,
on a single neon sign.
Here there's no price on heroes.
Better to ring for sleep.

So the mercy of a needle
brings me to a rough landing:
the rubbish men are loading
unspeakable detritus,
crashing with cheerful shouts
through a freezing mortal morning.

And the bank, no doubt for reasons
of economy, has turned
its symbol off. The crescent
moon and the morning star
over the Lands Department
fade into greater light.

MORNING AGAIN

Morning again, though not yet light.
The next-door bantams call me up
in a strange world where dream and waking
melt in a featureless expanse.

Some time of violence has been close.
No relics mark that endless plain,
but someone's buried, some new ghost
between one cockcrow and the next

is fretting. Now a figure rises
so distant one can only tell
from its stretched arms it might be human,
and, close behind, another presence

not human marks its stumbling flight;
cloudy enough to blur the line
of any possible horizon
yet like enough to all I fear

for me to know I am the human
figure with aching arms extended,
casting no shadow, reaching out,
for substance in my flight from terror.

Safety: calm light on leaf and feather
Here is the news. And now, the weather —
an ordinary human shadow
attends me as I fill the kettle.

BLACKBIRD

In the morning my blackbird sings
        "Believe in the Trinity."
In the evening he seems to say
        "Abandon all property."
Song, faith and ethics from one beak —
        what a divinity!

VISITOR

What light beguiles our dreams?
Does it keep Einsteinian laws?
How did your ashes seize
light, form, a speaking voice?

Are you ready now for my dream
in birdsong, lessening darkness?
Too late: you should have come
as once you came at midnight:

three days your newborn death
crazed me with nightmare howling.
You touched me. "I am come
from the grave to comfort you."

I slept in consolation
deeper than any sorrow.
Half-waking at my window
I rub my eyes, and see

a shadow cast by dreamlight
reflected in still water.
A heron stands unmoving,
a real bird on the rim

of an actual pond, possessing
somehow the selfsame space
(so music fills the body)
as your image in the dream.

You stare in ash-grey light,
pure dream of purer shadow,
then lift away, your voice
hungry and harsh.
                    All day

motions of thought are shaped
by curving wing, strict feather,
windstroke on ribs of water,
deathmask of clouded sky.

Which bird among the many
waiting stone-quiet with hunger
in leaden shallows came
to the threshold of my dream?

THE SUN DESCENDING

To the memory of Vera Cottew

I have the Oxford Blake you left me;
hold it as if to bring you close.
Walk with me where the old houses
offer their frogs and gnomes and artless
flower-filled swans made of bald tyres.
It will soon be night. The gutter's pouring
quicksilver and a broken bottle
glitters like Cinderella's slipper.

You loved the first of everything:
first breath of any season, first
light on anything, first blossom
on any bush, brush-stroke on canvas.

Half a lifetime, and I am holding
your favourite book, dark blue and gold.
Your spirit brushes mine. You walk
under the shining heavenly shell
with me, clean through the solid world.

CROW-CALL

"He lives eternally who lives in the present"
— Wittgenstein, Tractatus 6.4311

Let this be eternal life:
light ebbing, my dinghy drifting
on watershine, dead centre
of cloud and cloud-reflection —
high vapour, mind's illusion.

And for music, Baron Corvo,
my half-tame forest raven
with his bad leg unretracted
beating for home, lamenting
or, possibly, rejoicing
that he saw the world at all.

Space of a crow-call, enclosing
the self and all it remembers.
Heart-beat, wing-beat, a moment.
My line jerks taut. The cod
are biting. This too is eternal:
the death of cod at twilight.
And this: food on my table
keeping a tang of ocean.

So many, in raven darkness.
Why give death fancy names?

Corvo, where have you settled
your crippled leg for the night?

SCHRÖDINGER'S CAT PREACHES TO THE MICE

To A.D. Hope

Silk-whispering of knife on stone,
due sacrifice, and my meat came.
Caressing whispers, then my own
choice among laps by leaping flame.

What shape is space? Space will put on
the shape of any cat. Know this:
my servant Schrödinger is gone
before me to prepare a place.

So worship me, the Chosen One
in the great thought-experiment.
As in a grave I will lie down
and wait for the Divine Event.

The lid will close. I will retire
from sight, curl up and say Amen
to geiger counter, amplifier,
and a cylinder of HCN.

When will the geiger counter feel
decay, its pulse be amplified
to a current that removes the seal
from the cylinder of cyanide?

Dead or alive? The case defies
all questions. Let the lid be locked.
Truth, from your little beady eyes,
is hidden. I will not be mocked.

Quantum mechanics has no place
for what's there without observation.
Classical physics cannot trace
spontaneous disintegration.

If the box holds a living cat
no scientist on earth can tell.
But I'll be waiting, sleek and fat.
Verily, all will not be well

if, to the peril of your souls,
you think me gone. Know that this house
is mine, that kittens by mouse-holes
wait, who have never seen a mouse.

NIGHT AND DREAMS

I

"I come to you in a dream of ages
past," sings Crab. He swirls his velvet-
seaweed cloak. "When first we met,
and last, you will recall, I was
imprisoned in your father's house."

Sea colours on his carapace,
wave-hiss, tide-rustle in his voice.
"Some fiend had tied my fearful claws —"
— Yes, I recall. I must have been
a skinny child of eight or nine

that night my father brought you home —
"No, let *me* tell," says Crab, "this is
my aria, *my* party piece.
Grandmother, mother, father, brother
and you, went to the local theatre

leaving me bound in parching darkness.
I prayed: Redeemer Crab, release me
by your own sidelong righteousness
from these straightforward evildoers.
Take me where my transparent children

float in their manifold sea vision.
Silence. Mouse-whisper, cockroach-scuffle.
I felt, not far, the Brisbane River
ebbing to salt creek, mangrove swamp,
and burst my bonds, O yes I did!

and raged through your dark house, and hid.
That night you dared not go to bed
finding me gone when you returned.
Splintered pencils and toys proclaimed
my ocean strength. How soon forgotten

what Stan and Olly did and said!
Time, time. I felt the tide returning
far off. O Salt Redeemer, come
(I prayed) let navies drown to feed me
with rotten stump, decaying belly,

or if I am to die, allow me
one crunchbone tender-balancing foot."
— My father caught you. "Ah, he did.
'We'll cook the brute tonight,' he said.
'Bring me the hatpin.' Someone put

a diamond eye on a steel stalk
into your father's hand to stab
my stalked eyes. O the blaze of pain
eclipsing light's immense mandala!
Seagreen, seablue, I raged to red.

Boiling, crab died. I became Crab."

II

Crab is dressed for the feast: on lettuce shredded
to seaweed ribbons, cracked claws reassembled,
he lies among parsley curls and radish roses.
Our starchy Sunday-snowy cloth is set
with what remains of Greatgrandmother's china,
translucent white, rimmed with a deepsea blue.
On his great serving dish Crab's at the centre

of a splendid colour wheel: cucumber slices,
tomato, celery, carrot, egg: my work,
duly admired. My grandmother says grace.
"Where would you eat like this," my father asks,
passing the homemade bread, "except in Queensland?"
A lovely room. Windows give on the garden
rose and green panes of bubble-glass enchanting
the dullest day. The sideboard mirror offers
more light. Such light, restoring, recomposing
many who dined here. Most of them are dead.

III

"That's enough of pentameters,"
says Crab, returning to my dream.
— What shall I write, I ask. He writes,
so I won't miss his fearful joke:
THE DIRE BELLY VARIATIONS!

Making himself a cairn of stones
he says, "This is my own rock group.
O I'm the original punk rocker
with a hatpin through my brain, my brain,
with a diamond hatpin through my brain."

— Your jokes are awful. "I know worse."
— Impossible. "Shall I rehearse
the names of those who've died from cancer?
O I'm the original merry prankster,
a diamond hatpin's all my eye.

Tell me, where are those who ate
my claws, my tender body meat?
Laurel and Hardy fans, long gone!
You cracked my hardware, ate my software.
Now I'm programmed in your brain."

IV

More and more of the great questions,
such as: what am I doing here
in gumboots and a summer nightdress
in a moonlit garden chasing sheep?

The sheep are out. It's not a dream.
I'll mend the broken fence tomorrow.
What's left of night? Enough to dream in.
What dreams will come? Who else but Crab.

I ate him sixty years ago.
Ocean of memory, transposing
feaster and feast. He beckons, wearing
seaweed clothes, with sidelong charm.

"Shall we go to a pirate movie?"
— You like the sea? "I like the bodies,
and 'Take the lady below and make
her comfortable', that's what I like.

I can't be bothered with the love scenes.
I've opened hearts. I know what's in them."
At interval he buys refreshments,
"Two seafood sticks. One without crab.

Come live with me and be my supper
where colours have no boundaries,
where every word is writ in water,
I'll put my arm around your waist.

I'll put my armour round your waist.
Shell after shell my soft self waxes.
Seek help! Sea kelp for drowning sailors.
Great questions all have wavering answers."

Ghosts crowd to hear. O my lost loves.
Waking to hard-edge sunlit colours,
sharp birdsong, lamb-bleat, I recall
myself among the moonlit sheep

questioning — what? Why should I care
how long ago my death began?
Am I a ghost dreaming I'm human
with herbs to plant, a fence to mend?

THE MAGIC LAND OF MUSIC

I doubted from the beginning
that music was universal.
My mother was always arranging
matinees, soirees, functions
at which, in those innocent days
when even the wireless was rare,
her musical friends performed.

There was one called Irmtraud, who played
only largo and molto adagio;
any slow movement that didn't
divide beyond semiquavers
she rendered langsam und sehnsuchtsvoll
while her fidgeting rivals rolled
their eyeballs in utter boredom.

My mother sang sharp to my father's
accompaniment; my father,
whose ear was perfect, complained.
I had a particular loathing
for my teacher's favourite, Czerny.
Everybody loathed somebody
sometime, in the land of music.

I had one pupil who wished
to learn only De Camptown Ladies
and learned it, and quit for good,
and a boyfriend who told me crisply
"For Godsake don't play me Lieder"
replaced by another who wanted
Für Elise ad infinitum.

I heard the perhaps apocryphal
tale of a talented girl
with absolute pitch, growing up
in the backblocks with a deaf mother,
the piano so out of tune
that the child was riddled for life
and couldn't make sense of music.

Now I wonder what will remain
of our art in the nuclear winter.
What music will rise from the ruins?
Rodents, they say, will survive,
cockroach and scorpion flourish.
But only the wind will howl
langsam und sehnsuchtsvoll.

LONG AFTER HEINE

The washing machine was chuffing
    Ja-PAN Ja-PAN Ja-PAN
as she hustled her husbands townwards
    and her lonely day began.

The baby screamed with colic
    the windows streamed with rain.
She dreamed of a demon lover
    like Richard Chamberlain.

He towered, austerely perfect
    in samurai brocade,
and hushed the howling baby
    with one swish of his blade.

And then ... And then she rested,
    stroking the cruel sword
while he recited haiku
    and conjured word by word

a thatch of morning glory;
    a swallow's shadow cast
across the paper shutters;
    a snail stripped to the waist;

a fan seller dispensing
    coolness in summer heat;
a fly under the flyswat
    wringing his hands and feet;

a kingfisher's wet feathers
    catching the setting sun;
a field of summer grasses,
    the warrior's vision gone.

The cherry blossoms leaving
    a world of grief and pain.
A lonely woman sitting
    by glass lacquered with rain.

1945

Nineteen forty-five. I have been sick
all the way from Brisbane; first time in the air.
My husband's waiting in civilian clothes.
Another name now. All those burning glances
cancelled, all those raging letters burned.
And my mocking friends — "Holy MaTRIMony!"
"You've had your wings trimmed. You'll be Mother Goose."

We melt with good old-fashioned happiness
at the desolate terminal. I see the city
ending in bush, St George's on the skyline,
KEENS CURRY on the hill. We find a cafe.
"Lunch is off. Afternoon tea's not on,"
the waitress snaps, and sniffs. She knows we're strangers.
Saturday afternoon. How doth the city

sit solitary. A shuttered delicatessen
proclaims HIGH GRADE AND CONTINENTAL FOODSTUFFS.
What continent? Perhaps they mean the mainland.
I'm in my summer clothes. A wind breathes cold
truth in those English trees that tried to fool me
with their false fronts on a tourist office poster.
Know'st thou the land wherein the citrons bloom?

I do. Exile's the name I give that knowledge.
Even as I say How Beautiful How Charming
why do I feel that some demonic presence
hovers where too much evil has been done
near the harmless rivulet, the Georgian buildings?
Hungry, we link our lives and wait for evening.
In my husband's luggage the *Tractatus* waits

with the world that was the case already fading.

RESURRECTION

Night-coolness on glittering pasture
still, as my grandmother came
from her watch by a dying neighbour.

She sleepless, and I with my dreams
wide open to quickening day
as I fidgeted under the hairbrush:

"Her soul has taken flight."
I thought of a humanoid bird
flapping off above sounds of daybreak,

Willie Wagtail, poultry-bicker,
axe-echo, rattle of trace-chains,
to perch on God's golden throne.

— Are we doing some fowls today?
"No, today's not a day for killing,
my dear. Go and catch the butcher."

So I waved to his cart from the gate
where an elderly rooster, reprieved,
crowed up his second-last morning.

The pick of the cart! He cut
our joint; heavy carcasses swung
from the roof as he trimmed and grunted,

"So the dippy old maid has kicked it!"
My grandmother frowned rebuke.
"Our *neighbour* has *gone to heaven*."

With the rudeness permitted to one
whose wife was flighty, he barked,
"Don't give me the resurrection!

Those millions! It stands to reason
there wouldn't be space to hold them.
there simply wouldn't be room!"

I saw pig-pale bodies depending
from hooks in their jaws, and God
with a knife in bilious light

distracted: "No room! No room!"
But my grandmother, counting her change,
said, "Remember God isn't a butcher,

as time will tell."
                    I am older
than she was then. Time has told me
less than I need to know.

If eternal life can be given
let me have it again as a child
among those whom I did not love

enough, while they lived. Let me wake,
if I wake at all, on the threshold
of day in my father's house

believing all riddles have answers
night gone   my grandmother walking
head bowed   over glittering pasture.

MID-CHANNEL

"The days shall come upon you, that he will take you away with hooks, and your posterity with fishhooks"
— Amos, IV, 2

Cod inert as an old boot,
tangling dance of the little shark,
perch nibble, flathead jerk —
blindfold I'd know them on my line.

Fugitive gleam on scale and fin,
lustrous eye, opalescent belly
dry and die in the undesired
element. A day will come,

matter-of-fact as knife and plate,
with death's hook in my jaw, and language
unspeakable, the line full out.
I'll tire you with my choking weight

old monster anchored in the void.
My God, you'll wonder what you've caught.
Land me in hell itself at last
I'll stab and swell your wounds with poison.

Not here, not now. Water's my kingdom
tonight, my line makes starspecks tremble.
The dinghy's decked with golden eyes
and still the cod boil round my bait.

NIGHT THOUGHTS

"Hell is for those who doubt that hell exists."
One of the elohim with whom I fight
from 4 a.m. to cockcrow, told me this.
He hit me in the thigh for emphasis.
Is it a dream? If so, the dream persists.

I meet him always at the edge of night.
He knows me, but he'll never give his name.
Why should you know, he says. I have to guess
whether he comes to punish or to bless.
I thought once he was death, but at first light

he goes, and I get up. Things are the same
as usual. The sounds of day begin:
the kettle and the news; so it's not death
who comes in the small hours to cramp my breath.
Sleep is extinguished like a candle flame.

Longing for peace I wrestle, try to pin
the adversary down. Tell me your name.
Tell me, did language lapse when mankind fell?
Tell me, is "He descended into hell"
a metaphor? The literal truth? Where in

this universe could hell be? He persists:
"Hell is for those who doubt that hell exists."

MIDWINTER

Midwinter and the treasures of the snow
fall as chill rain on Salamanca Market.
A day for a good book, and here's a bargain:
a commentary on the Book of Job.
Queensland Book Depot, Albert Street. O Brisbane

have you sent me this text, and to what end,
from my old lunch-hour haunt, how have you found me?
Speak, memory: a red-haired child is sitting
beside her grandmother, who's busy sewing
braid on her son-in-law's Masonic apron.

I'd heard about my father's God, the Great
Architect of the Universe, a being
served by his menfolk in their fancy aprons.
My mother's God rode on her hip, the boy-child
to whom she sang, at whom she smiled all day.

My father's house: a small War Service cottage,
verandas back and front, a fruitful acre
with horse, cow, ducks and fowls, an orange orchard,
a neat path leading through the fenced-off peas.
"A path," my father grinned, "which no fowl knoweth."

"Read to me, my dear." I want my comics,
but Tiger Tim and Jolly Joking Jumbo
will have to wait. The place is marked in Job.
Gold, crystal, sapphire, onyx, topaz, rubies —
I know the jewels by heart, but wisdom's better.

My grandmother was born in eighteen-eighty.
Married at seventeen and widowed early
she loved her native Queensland, and the future
in the shadow of God's hand did not confound her
in a world where good and evil grew together.

She used one text as if it were a charm:
"Though he slay me, yet will I trust in him."
I see that's an inspired mistranslation
of "He will slay me. I will wait for him.
Lo, he will kill me, and I will not hope."

I will be slain, but with my face towards him.
Is that why we like games? Who'd go to matches
if the full forwards lay down? Wrestle with angels!
Now at three-score and ten, I seem to live
most of the time in existential terror.

I think of Hume, modest philosopher,
approaching death "composed in mind, and free
from anxiety, impatience or low spirits,"
and of my grandmother (who'd never read him)
accepting age and illness in that spirit.

One a great sceptic, one a true believer.
He'd have liked her. He took particular pleasure
in the company, he said, of modest women.
When Job is questioned, snow is ranked with death,
with the morning stars, and lightning, and Leviathan.

Snow settles on the mountain as I read.
If death prove an experience I live through,
good angel, guide me to a sunlit kitchen
with bread rising, the great black kettle singing
of wisdom and the peaceful life to come.

"THIS ARTIFICE OF AIR"

Poems of Love and Death

I

Dazed by your celestial height
I summon you by name: sustain me,
Father Aether, hold me firm.
Virtuoso of high clouds
come down from your solitudes,
come in your outlandish crimson,
fold me in your evening arms
safely out of tweaking reach
of tightly-buttoned Little Masters.
Let me be your golden child.
Teach me with your tongue of lightning
polynomial enchantment.
Sweet Sir Aether, set your hands
on my hipbones, here and here,
swear at dead of night we'll lie
in one another's arms and die.

II

Nature, they often say, is never new.
I doubt it, looking at that ancient crow,
frayed hunchback on a bushfire-blackened limb.
He'll never see the ducklings' kingdom come
though he's breakfasted on egg.
                                                My death has been
promised by water in a true friend's dream.
I'll come again to shore, my bones picked clean
by seaweed-mantled crabs, and ground to grit,
dividend of the tempests underfoot
of crows maybe, or lovers, or Chanticleer
to whom I'm given as shellgrit.
                                                Only swear
you'll mourn me, old and dying, whip the rough
waters to a grand Wagnerian huff —
Goldenchild's Liebestod.
                                        Crow takes to air.
In curdled mist his lumbering ghost cries: SWEAR.

III

Father Aether and Goldenchild
        were floating side by side,
far from the land whose heavy law
        they could not long abide.
They laughed like anything to see
        the light foam on the tide.

"Phantasmagoric love, how shall
        we spend this holy day?"
said Goldenchild — "dive with the tern,
        or join in dolphin play,
or make a cloudy song to chase
        aetherial blues away?

Or shall we spend a thoughtful hour
        talking philosophy?"
"Like any child, you talk too much."

(He rocked her on the sea.)
"Your wits belong to Wittgenstein,
but your body belongs to me.

Lie quiet, lie still my Goldenchild,
and I will sing to you,
your eyelids closed in peace, your breast
expanding to the blue,
I have my book of Ancient Airs,
but none of these will do.

I'll sing that long night when we lay
together in a dream,
and I danced at daybreak in high boots
in tussocky greenshine-gleam.
My music at your waking fled,
but you shall hear that theme."

He sang. From heaven streamed an air
so ravishing and mild
that visions lost by night, and waking
dreams were reconciled,
and strangers in drab alien streets
at welcoming faces smiled.

HERONGATE

To Graeme Hetherington

I dream I am opening the door
of Herongate lost in the fire,
gone into the world of light
in one way or another, if dreams
are as real as anything else.

In the dream the house is intact,
a world without metaphor, standing
foursquare, with its ramshackle shed
and its tanks and wreathing geraniums.
So all is well, after all,

until I look down at my hand,
at my fingers turning the key:
my bones are as white as a long-bleached shell,
as smooth, as beautiful.
I have died. It was I who died

and have come in my dream to this door,
a skeleton in a summer dress,
whose dream was fire, whose language
must manage without any tongue
of fire, or anything else.

And what will my fingers write
without sinew or flesh, though the bones
by some strange gravitational force
that seems to be partial to dactyls
are turning my key in the lock.

O my bird-haunted shack in the dunes!
A nest that I shaped to myself.
There are streets I can't cross for the ghosts,
but in Paradise nothing can happen.
Alone, I invested in silence,

except for the resident possums.
I hope they escaped from the fire.
This hope marks the edge of my dream
as I wake in the city, alive.
Far off, a faint bloom in the marshes

is announcing a change of season,
and perhaps an invisible presence
that does not startle the herons
cries out by the desolate tankstands
to purge its grief, is waiting

like a satyr straight out of Isaiah
with the cormorant and the bittern
possessing the stones of emptiness
until I return, to tell me
my days will not be prolonged.

WITTGENSTEIN'S SHOEBOX

Tell me, ye powers that dwell below,
how did this shoebox come to be
on a stall in Salamanca market?

Are they philosophers approaching?
No, clergymen. I needn't worry.
Fifty cents, and it's mine for ever.

The box is crammed with paper slips:
mixed-up observations, thoughts
on the origins of human language.

> Think of a language where each word
> is used and understood once only.
> Leaf-drift of useless syllables!
>
> If a cane toad could be taught to speak
> how could we know if it were lying?
> Think of the neural infrastructure.

Here's the man himself. He wants his box back.
"Ludwig —" He scowls. "Herr Wittgenstein,
has the verb *to dream* a present tense?"

I tell him, "Once I saw a raven
eating chips from a paper bag
on a high branch of this very plane tree.

Corvus tasmanicus. Believe me."
He doesn't and the paper strips
fly up and deck the tree with leaves.

I wake, as always, with my problems
unsolved. It's true about the raven.
I can bring you a living witness.

LATER TEXTS

I

She sits in the park, wishing she'd never written
about that dowdy housewife and her brood.
Better, the Memoirs of a Mad Sex-Kitten,
or a high-minded Ode to Motherhood
in common metre with a grand doxology.
"They have eaten me alive." Did she write that?
The sonnet nestles in a new anthology
safe in its basket as a favoured cat.

She sits a while in flickering light rehearsing
the family's birthdays. "Stop, you bloody fool!"
A young house-father with a pram is cursing
a child who's pushed another in the pool.
She helps him calm them. "Eating you alive?
Look at me. I've lived through it. You'll survive."

II

She practises a fugue for pure enjoyment,
the graceful C sharp major from Book One.
Friends call. "Still at your classical employment?"
She plays it through for them. The setting sun
blazes on a brass owl, a grandchild's present.
Owls are not passerines. The claws are wrong.
They sit with drinks. She shows them an unpleasant
poison-pen letter. "Where does this belong?"

"Why not donate it to a library?
Give the anonymous pest one taste of fame.
Make work for a detective PhD."
They talk of absent friends, and what became
of children (middle-aged now), and the past.
Be wise, my sorrow. Evening falls at last.

III

Eloisa to Abelard

Believe me, here behind the veil all's well.
Less work, more time for reading. Writing, too.
Eventually one leaves Heartbreak Hotel.
So, how are things? I sometimes think of you,
Sweetheart, and now and then I wonder what
Topics you lecture on. Still keen on Bede?
Historia Calamitatum's not
Everyone's title. Still, it's a good read.
Expect you'll sell a few. I hope to put
Down a few thoughts in writing. About us.
I hear you're up for heresy. Appeal
To Rome, why don't you? Bernard needs the boot,
Or swatting with *De Intellectibus*.
Rock on, old love. I know just how you feel.

THE OWL AND THE PUSSYCAT BAUDELAIRE ROCK

You longed for night and the night is coming,
the rays of the daystar fade and die,
the nightwind rises, the tide is waiting,
and the years that are gone lean down from the sky.
Baby my baby, I'll love you forever,
when your head's burned out and your light's all gone,
my eyes will find you in stony darkness.
Baby my baby the night comes on.

Rock on, rock on till we reach that country
where all is harmony and delight,
fragrance of amber, fathomless mirrors
reflecting the gold and hyacinth light.
Baby my baby I'll love you forever,
when your brain's ground out and your dreams are gone
I'll hunt you out through seas of darkness.
Baby my baby the night comes on.

Rock on, rock on, my songs enfold you,
        the moon slides down and the water's wild,
the snowpeaks gleam on the far horizon,
        the sun will rise like a golden child.
        You asked for night and look it is falling
        your peace is here, your sorrow is gone,
        lie at my side in the rocking darkness.
        Baby my baby, the night comes on.

LATE WORKS

Time to think of your Late Works
in the pure daylit atmosphere
of mystical acceptance, freedom
from old monsters, etcetera.

Time to be calmly transcendental
and abstract, time to set the stakes
so high no one will bet on you,
fill any form with stuff that breaks

the form so everything pours out
in a Great Fugue no one can play.
All those you wanted to impress
are dead or sick or pretty crazy

and those you know will understand it
are not yet born. Nurse, I need paper.
No, not that kind, you idiot girl,
the kind you write on. Get me Matron,

Matron I need a fountain pen.
If you have any wits about you
they're PhDs requesting access
to things you can't remember writing

to people you don't now remember.
Time to make light of time. Forget it.
Look through it. Write those late great works.
What was it that you asked the nurse for?

No matter now. You have your life
before you, you're a child enjoying
your self, the unity of contrasts.
Whose hand is it that holds your pen?

Gwen Harwood, one of Australia's most celebrated poets and librettists, published more than 420 works in her lifetime, many of which continue to be studied widely in schools and universities across Australia. She has won the Officer of the Order of Australia (AO), the Victorian Premier's Literary Award and the Patrick White Award. She died in 1995, aged seventy-five.

www.ingramcontent.com/pod-product-compliance
Lightning Source LLC
Chambersburg PA
CBHW021329060726
47591CB00006B/1942

* 9 7 8 1 7 6 0 6 4 3 6 5 2 *